GRANADA 1492
THE RECONQUEST OF SPAIN

GRANADA 1492
THE RECONQUEST OF SPAIN

WRITTEN BY
DAVID NICOLLE PhD

BATTLESCENE ARTWORK BY
ANGUS McBRIDE

First published in Great Britain in 1998 by Osprey Publishing, Elms Court, Chapel Way, Botley, Oxford OX2 9LP, United Kingdom.
Email: info@ospreypublishing.com

Also published as Campaign 53 Granada 1492

ISBN 1 84176 111 7

Editor: Ian MacGregor
Designer: Luise Roberts

Colour bird's eye view illustrations by Peter Harper
Cartography by Micromap
Battlescene artwork by Angus McBride
Filmset in Singapore by Pica Ltd.
Printed in China through World Print Ltd.

FOR A CATALOGUE OF ALL BOOKS PUBLISHED BY OSPREY MILITARY AND AVIATION PLEASE WRITE TO:

The Marketing Manager, Osprey Direct USA, PO Box 130, Sterling Heights, MI 48311-0130, USA.
Email: info@ospreydirectusa.com

The Marketing Manager, Osprey Direct UK, PO Box 140, Wellingborough, Northants, NN8 4ZA, United Kingdom.
Email: info@ospreydirect.co.uk

Visit Osprey at:
www.ospreypublishing.com

Key to Military Series symbols

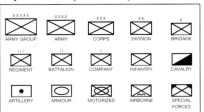

Dedication

For Arwed Ulrich Koch, who shed light on the Moors.

FRONT COVER: Courtesy of David Nicolle

BACK COVER: The Alhambra Palace, Granada (courtesy of David Nicolle)

PAGE 2 **A section of the well known painting of St Dominic presiding over an *Auto da Fé*, or burning of heretics, by the Spanish artist Pedro Berruguete.(Prado, Madrid)**

TITLE PAGE **One of the two war swords of King Fernando of Aragon. This magnificent late 15th century weapon is in an Iberian-Islamic tradition associated with light cavalry combat *a la jinete*. (Inv. G.31, Real Armeria, Madrid).**

CONTENTS

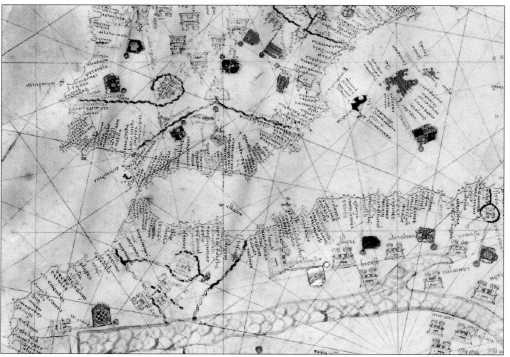

THE ORIGINS OF THE CAMPAIGN

THE CHRISTIAN KINGDOMS BEFORE 1480

LEFT **The castle of Salobreña on the coast of what was the Amirate of Granada. In typical Andalusian fashion the fortress was built on a rock and is surrounded by a fertile *vega* or intensively cultivated area. (Author's photograph)**

BELOW **The Alcazabar or citadel of the Alhambra Palace overlooking Granada. A round artillery bastion built in the 15th century can be seen on the left. (Author's photograph)**

LEFT **Section from a chart made in 1413 showing southern Spain and North-west Africa. These *portalan* maps were designed to help plan naval journeys so they provide much more information about coasts than inland areas. (*Hocia de Villadeste Portalan Map*, Res. Ge AA 566, Bibliothèque Nationale, Paris)**

Long before the fall of Granada in 1492, Castilian ambitions were growing and already looked beyond the Iberian peninsula. Dreams of conquering Morocco, for example, stretched back as far as the 13th century. The struggle against Islam within Spain and Portugal was, of course, far older. It was political as well as religious, and the centuries of what are now called the Reconquista gave Spanish Christianity a warlike character. The Reconquista also resulted in a powerful Marian Cult in the frontier regions, with captured mosques often being rededicated to the Virgin Mary, often in association with other saints. The Virgin was also believed to be present during battles against the Moors, as the Arabic-speaking Muslim inhabitants of Iberia were then called. In the conquered territories, new churches and monasteries were also built over old *ribâts*, the places where devout Muslims lived a religious life and fought for their faith. Similarly, new Christian saints 'took over' from previous Muslim holy men, and as a result Moors and *mudejars* (Muslims living under Christian rule) might revere a Christian shrine on the grounds that its saint was *'a relative of the Prophet Muhammad'*.

In complete contrast to this blurring of religious identities, the 15th century saw growing intolerance towards Muslims, Jews and above all 'heretics' throughout Spain. As a result, both the Inquisition, which came to Spain in 1478, and the war against Granada were widely popular. Religious persecution also had a political purpose, with the rulers of Castile and Aragon using the Inquisition as a tool to impose modern concepts of national unity. The first to feel the heat were the *Conversos*, mostly Jewish families which had converted to Christianity in earlier decades but retained various distinctive social habits. Only later did the Jews themselves and the Muslims become direct targets of official persecution. Given this feverish atmosphere and the unfinished business of the Reconquista, it is hardly surprising that the defeat of the Moors featured prominently in popular Spanish culture. In Andalusia re-enactments of the triumph of Christianity often

ended with the actor playing the Muslim Prophet Muhammad being thrown into the village fountain, while the diabolical and sexual perversions attributed to Muslims fuelled fear and hatred.

The area of Castile most immediately involved in this struggle was Andalusia. The fertile Guadalquivir valley with the once Islamic cities of Cordoba and Seville had never really recovered from Christian conquest in the 13th century and it remained underpopulated following large-scale expulsions of the original Muslim inhabitants, although a large Muslim minority of *mudejars* remained. At the top of the social tree were

'*The Battle of Clavijo*', in a print by the German artist Martin Schongauer. Schongauer is believed to have visited Spain in the mid-15th century, which would account for the remarkable accuracy of his portrayal of both Spanish warriors and Moorish soldiers. (Inv. B-14150, National Gallery of Art, Washington)

grandee families descended from the leaders of the Reconquista. Then there were 'new' aristocratic families dating from the 14th century, while the cities were dominated by entrenched political oligarchies. The crown and grandees competed for the allegiance of the lesser nobility who formed local military élites. Further east, the kingdom of Murcia formed part of the Castilian realm but, as a wedge of territory on the Mediterranean coast between Christian Aragon and Muslim Granada, retained a somewhat separate identity.

Some Castilian cities in Andalusia had a 'noble' corporate status, while others did not. They ranged from sleepy Cordoba to bustling Seville, which already looked to overseas territories in the Canary Islands and beyond. Other cities like Jerez were little more than country towns, although they were proud of their role as military centres facing Granada and of their skilled militias. Towns and villages close to the frontier were generally exempt from central government taxation, though many were under the direct protection of the crown rather than one of the grandee families. But in return for this privileged position, they defended the frontier, maintained communications, repaired fortifications, and took part in raids. One of the crown's most effective weapons in its quarrels with the grandees was the Santa Hermandad, an urban league which provided reliable militias. Around Seville earlier in the 15th century, for example, King Juan II had used Seville's militia to gain control over numerous surrounding castles.

Within this turbulent world noble families had a strong sense of continuity, a characteristic which extended to the *bando*, a political faction or party which in turn included families who were not directly related to the local aristocracy. Many *bandos* also drew in the urban oligarchies, all sharing a concept of communal loyalty which stemmed from the Islamic past, their young men having learnt military skills, as well as the traditions of the *bando*.

Another focus of Andalusian military and political power were the Military Orders of Santiago, Calatrava and Alcantara which had large estates and numerous frontier castles. Seville was already looking far beyond southern Spain for its wealth and power, having been a great

Atlantic port under Islamic rule. Many of Seville's 'masters of ships' were royal officials, but some grandee families were also involved in Atlantic exploration and trade.

The situation in Aragon was different to that in Castile. It was much less feudal, more urbanised and outward looking – though towards the Mediterranean rather than the Atlantic. In fact Aragon already had an overseas empire in southern Italy. Unlike Castile, the cities and the Church were more powerful in Aragon than the nobility. The Mediterranean coast and the fertile Ebro valley in the north had also been the second 'heartland' of old Muslim al-Andalus: there were large Muslim *mudejar* minorities in many areas, while trade links with Muslim North Africa were strong. One thing Aragon and Castile shared in the late 15th century was their rulers' determination to impose royal authority throughout their kingdoms.

The Papacy in Rome had, earlier in the 15th century, shown a revived interest in Crusading, primarily directed against Ottoman Turks in the Balkans. This enthusiasm spread to Spain and the war against Muslim Granada. Indulgences were offered, taxes were raised in support of the Christian cause, and volunteers were encouraged to fight beneath the banners of Castile and Aragon. Border warfare between Christians and Muslims had developed its own, very distinctive character in southern

ABOVE **A donor figure on the painted altar-piece of St Vicente de Fora attributed to Nuno Gonçalves, Portuguese 1450-1500. The Portuguese clung to many Moorish fashions long after they had been abandoned elsewhere. (National Museum of Ancient Art, Lisbon)**

LEFT **The Torre del Homenaje of the Alhambra. Beyond is the Torre de las Gillinas. (Author's photograph)**

RIGHT **The Torre del Peinador of the Alhambra Palace, seen from the Torre de Comares or 'Tower of the North African volunteers'. These include sumptuous pavilions where the inhabitants of the Nasrid palace could enjoy a magnificent view across the fertile *vega* to the mountains. (Author's photograph)**

Spain. Both sides accepted the concept of a frontier zone, but neither accepted that this frontier was static. The Christian side was dominated by the ideology of the unfinished Reconquista, while the Muslims fought for a belief in *jihad*, a holy war in defence of a beleaguered Islam. A war-like co-existence had developed, punctuated by raids and piracy, though relations were rarely stretched to breaking point. Once the internal problems of Castile and Aragon were solved, however, and the kingdoms were united through the marriage of their rulers, Granada's doom was ultimately sealed.

Life on the frontier was dominated by warfare and only those with an official *amân*, or safe conduct, could cross the border freely.

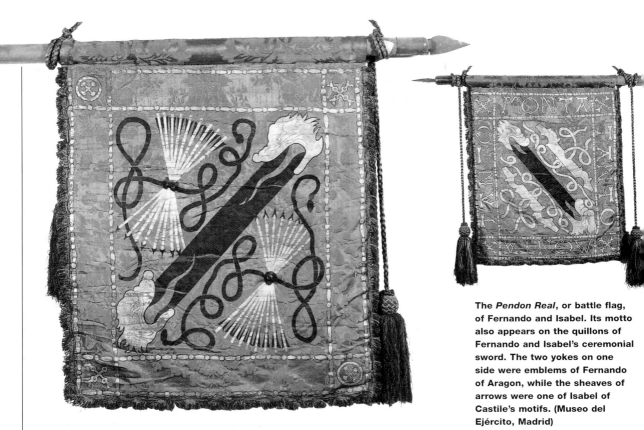

The *Pendon Real*, or battle flag, of Fernando and Isabel. Its motto also appears on the quillons of Fernando and Isabel's ceremonial sword. The two yokes on one side were emblems of Fernando of Aragon, while the sheaves of arrows were one of Isabel of Castile's motifs. (Museo del Ejército, Madrid)

Nevertheless there were plenty of instances of people changing sides in both directions, including members of the military élite. Both sides evolved similar patterns of military behaviour which were different from those seen elsewhere in western Europe. Border warfare itself ranged from the gentlemanly to the savage. Christian raiders habitually returned with the heads or ears of slain enemies, heads even being given to children for footballs, while on the Muslim side rewards were sometimes paid for enemy scalps. The ethos of border warfare was well portrayed in the epic *Tirant lo Blanc*, written in Catalonia in the mid-15th century. Here a Christian king insisted that his young son kill a captive Moor and then plunge his hand into the gushing wound, *'Thus baptising his son in infidel blood.'*

The senior Castilian officials in charge of cross-border relations, *Alcaldes entre cristianos y moros*, had plenty to do as cattle rustling and kidnapping were common. They had a corps of assistants called *fieles del rastro*, or in Murcia *ballesteros de monte*, charged with identifying culprits and returning property. Then there were the *Alfaqueques* who had a form of diplomatic immunity which enabled them to seek out prisoners and arrange their ransom or exchange. Senior men captured in battle were, in fact, usually ransomed by their government, while poor people could only hope to be exchanged, and this often involved complex financial negotiations with those holding prisoners. Captives did not always want to go home. In 1479, shortly before the outbreak of the final war, a young Christian prisoner converted to Islam and refused to leave until Muslim government officials arranged for his family to cross the frontier and convince him to leave. One woman had such a dubious reputation that neither side wanted her back! It was agreed that prisoners could escape if they were able, though they were not permitted to take stolen enemy property with them. The result was a close, though not exactly friendly, relationship between Christian and Muslim frontier communities.

THE AMIRATE OF GRANADA BEFORE 1480

Granada was full of the descendants of refugees who had fled from regions lost to the Spanish. It was also wealthy, with its élite owning villas in the fertile *vega*, or irrigated land. Society had never been feudal, but was dominated by castle-holding *qâ'ids*, many of these men being clan leaders. The social attitudes of such *qâ'id* families were, however, similar to those of the Spanish aristocracy. Otherwise society was organised in a sort of clan system of related families with personal status depending on wealth rather than lineage. In the densely populated Amirate of Granada, a great deal of food had to be imported from potentially hostile neighbours, so irrigated agriculture had become much more intensive. Many fertile *vegas* around towns and cities consisted of fruit orchards and mulberry trees to feed the silkworms upon which so much of the country's wealth depended. Yet this sort of agriculture also meant that the Granadan countryside was highly vulnerable to enemy raiders.

The Arabic spoken in Granada was a local dialect called *al-Gharbi* or 'western' which contained many Latin-based words. Many people on both sides of the frontier spoke both Spanish and Arabic, and despite their emphatic Islamic identity, the Muslims of Granada shared several festivals with their Christian neighbours. The mid-summer solstice, for example, known as St John's Day to Christians and *ansara* to the Muslims, was an occasion for military displays and tournaments on both sides of the border. This mixed heritage was also reflected in costume and military equipment. Consequently, the military élite of Granada often looked very different to their fellow Muslims in North Africa, but similar to their Spanish opponents.

The ruler of Granada was sometimes called the Amir, sometimes the Sultan, and his system of government was much the same as that seen

The 11th century *hamam*, or heated public baths in Granada. They were an essential part of life in a medieval Islamic city. (Author's photograph)

THE KINGDOM OF GRANADA AND IT'S NEIGHBOURS IN 1481

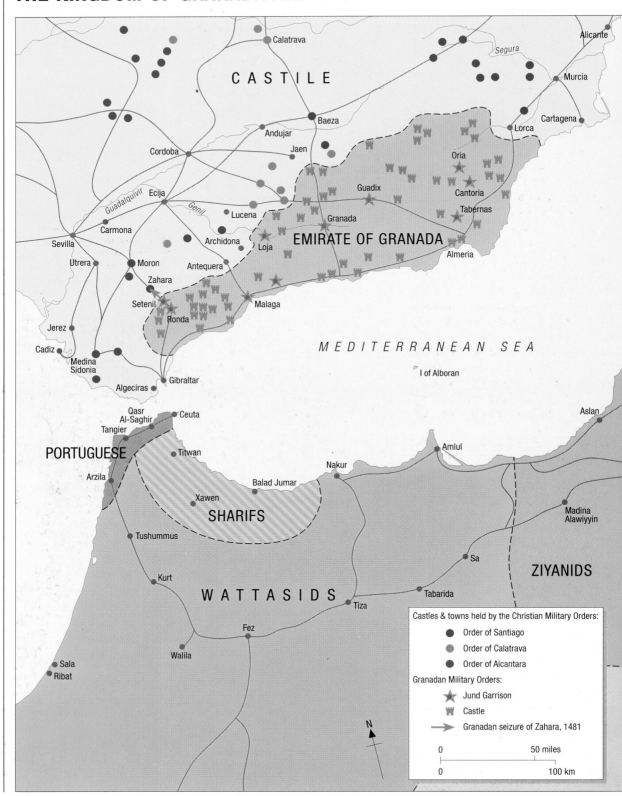

CASTILE

Calatrava
Alicante
Segura
Murcia
Baeza
Cartagena
Andujar
Lorca
Jaen
Oria
Cordoba
Guadix
Cantoria
Ecija
Tabernas
Guadalquivir
Genil
Lucena
Granada
Carmona
EMIRATE OF GRANADA
Sevilla
Archidona
Loja
Almeria
Utrera
Moron
Antequera
Zahara
Malaga
Setenil
Ronda
Jerez
MEDITERRANEAN SEA
Cadiz
I of Alboran
Medina
Sidonia
Algeciras
Gibraltar
Aslan
Qasr
Al-Saghir
Ceuta
Tangier
Amlul
PORTUGUESE
Titwan
Arzila
Nakur
Balad Jumar
Madina
Alawiyyin
Xawen
SHARIFS
Tushummus
Sa
ZIYANIDS
Kurt
Tabarida
WATTASIDS
Tiza
Fez
Walila
Sala
Ribat

Castles & towns held by the Christian Military Orders:

- Order of Santiago
- Order of Calatrava
- Order of Alcantara

Granadan Military Orders:

- ★ Jund Garrison
- Castle
- → Granadan seizure of Zahara, 1481

N

0	50 miles
0	100 km

everywhere else in the pre-modern Muslim world. Like the rulers of other threatened frontier states, the Amirs often had to raise higher taxes than were permitted under Islamic *Sharia* law, and the rulers of Granada were also vulnerable to criticism because of their relationship with neighbouring Castile. Paying tribute was no problem, especially as this was often disguised as gifts to a fellow ruler, but to become the vassal of an infidel king went against every principle of Islamic law. In fact, Granada stopped paying regular tribute in the late 14th century, and Castilian efforts to reimpose this duty in the 15th century are sometimes regarded as a major reason for the outbreak of the final war.

Granada's only real source of external support was North Africa, but once the Muslims lost control of the Strait of Gibraltar, this lifeline could be cut by the Christians. Militarily, Morocco was now in a very feeble state, its tribal armies fragmented and its navy a mere memory. North African volunteers still came to serve in Granada for religious reasons but direct Granadan military involvement in Morocco had ended with the failure of the joint Nasrid-Marînid attempt to retake Ceuta from the Portuguese in 1419. *Sufi shaykhs,* or leaders of slightly unorthodox religious brotherhoods, became the focus of resistance to Portuguese and Spanish involvement in North Africa, but were no real help to Granada.

Refugees from Granada poured into these areas before, during and after the final war, and brought more modern military ideas and weapons including firearms. In fact they contributed a great deal to the defeat of Christian invasions in the 15th and 16th centuries.

Nasrid Granada was wracked by political division much of the time. Amirs came and went, and came back again, while other ambitious families struggled for influence. Amongst these were the Banû al-Sarrâj who often dominated the *vizirate* or 'prime ministership' of Granada, and were generally regarded as pro-Castilian or anti-North African.

There was constant tension in Granadan society, with a general siege mentality in which the *jihâd* had wide appeal. Enthusiastic North African volunteers were a common sight, while the Nasrid army was remarkably large given the small size of the state. The country was densely fortified and by the late 15th century it was more common for the main *hisn* (castles) to have permanent gar-

Another donor figure on the painted altar-piece of St Vicente de Fora. He wears Andalusian-Islamic costume, including a local variation of the *qalansuwa* cap with a tassel, plus Moorish leather riding boots. (National Museum of Ancient Art, Lisbon)

risons than in earlier years. The most threatened frontier was to the north and north-west, while much of the bleak north-east consisted of a depopulated no-man's-land. Government officials were responsible both for frontier defence and for stopping minor incidents spiralling out of control, and peace-keeping systems were more centralised than on the Castilian side of the frontier. The treatment of prisoners varied, with many working mills or irrigation pumps, or building fortifications until they were ransomed or exchanged, though young men and boys were sometimes kept as soldiers of slave origin in a manner similar to the better-known *mamlûk* system of the Middle East.

ABOVE **The Puerta de los Leones of Toledo Cathedral built around 1460. The soldier touching the coffin or Ark in the centre is portrayed as a Moor and has a turban-cloth wound around his helmet. (Author's photograph)**

RIGHT **The Torres Bermejas which formed an outlying part of the fortifications of the Alhambra in Granada. It was originally linked to the main Alcazaba citadel by a long wall with towers facing in both directions. (Author's photograph)**

THE GATHERING STORM

By the late 15th century the existence of the Amirate of Granada was seen as an insult to the Christian Church, and under Queen Isabel the old idea of *convivencia*, co-existence, had given way to a determination to destroy this relic of Muslim power in the Iberian peninsula. Queen Isabel may have demanded King Fernando's help in return for the support she promised him for Aragon's ambitions in Italy. Perhaps Isabel and Fernando also felt the need for a successful Crusade to keep their own turbulent, warlike nobility content. Fernando and Isabel certainly used royalist propaganda, encouraging, for example, a belief that a king of Spain would one day conquer Granada, cross Africa, retake Jerusalem, destroy the religion of Islam, become the world's 'Last Emperor' and thus bring about Judgement Day. This 'Last Emperor' was given mystical names such as 'the Hidden One', 'the Bat' or 'the New David' – and many Spaniards believed that King Fernando was that man.

Fernando and Isabel certainly felt it necessary to justify their actions in religious terms in a letter to the Pope: *'We have not been moved to this war by any desire to enlarge our realms or seigneuries,... But our desire to serve God, and our zeal for His Holy Catholic faith, made us put all other interests aside and forget the constant travails and dangers which continue to increase for this cause..., hoping only that the Holy Catholic Faith will be multiplied and that Christendom will be quit of so constant a danger as she has here at our very doors, if these infidels of the Kingdom of Granada are not uprooted and cast out from Spain.'*

THE OPPOSING COMMANDERS

SPANISH LEADERS

The marriage of Fernando and Isabel united Aragon and Castile, the two largest Iberian kingdoms, under the rule of husband and wife. It was a fragile union, yet it survived Isabel's death in 1504 and formed the basis of the modern Spanish state.

King Fernando of Aragon was a remarkable ruler who may have been the model for Machiavelli's famous treatise on rulership, *The Prince*. His origins were mixed, and included ancestors who were *conversos* (Jews who had converted to Christianity), though this was largely kept quiet in the intolerant atmosphere of late 15th century Spain. Fernando himself was an astute diplomat, a fine and undoubtedly courageous soldier, but also a philanderer. The complex situation over which he ruled is shown in his titles or regnal numbers: he was Fernando II of Aragon and Sicily, Fernando V of Castile as a result of his marriage to Isabel, and Fernando III of Naples. Born in 1452, he married Isabel in 1469 and became king of Aragon in 1479. He and his wife retained control of their respective kingdoms but worked in close harmony where wider Spanish affairs such as the war in Granada were concerned. In 1494 Pope Alexander VI gave them the title of *Los Reyes Catolicos*, 'the Catholic Monarchs', and it was during their joint reign that Spain became one of Europe's foremost powers.

Isabel, Queen of Castile, did not command her armies in person, but was the prime mover and leading organiser of the final war against Granada. Born on 23 April 1451, she married Fernando of Aragon when she was 17 years of age. When her half-brother, Enrique IV of Castile, died in 1474, the Castilian nobility refused to accept the legitimacy of his young daughter, and so Isabel was crowned. Civil war followed, ending in Isabel's favour five years later. Though Isabel was an intolerant religious fanatic, she looked after her soldiers with an almost motherly care. As a result they loved her dearly and responded enthusiastically to her morale-boosting visits while on campaign. As Diego de Valera wrote to King Fernando in 1485, the Queen *'fights no less with her many alms and devout prayers than you, lord, with your lance in hand'*.

Much less is known about the secondary leaders of those armies which invaded Granada because they were so overshadowed by Fernando and Isabel. One of the most important was Enrique de Guzman, Duke of Medina Sidonia, Queen Isabel's viceroy in southern Castile. He was one of the leading grandees of the Seville area, having dominated the region since defeating his rival Poncé de Leon, Marquis of Cadiz. Yet Enrique de Guzman was more than an old-fashioned power-seeking medieval nobleman. He was an educated and outward looking man who invested money, time and effort in trading expeditions to the Canary Islands and Guinea. During the 1470s Enrique had protected the persecuted *conversos* of

BELOW **Part of the famous painting of St Dominic presiding over an *Auto da Fé*, or burning of heretics, by the Spanish artist Pedro Berruguete. The foot soldiers are equipped in southern Spanish Andalusian style, while the horseman is equipped as a light cavalryman *a la jinete*. (Prado, Madrid)**

'Resurrection', on an anonymous panel painting made between 1450 and 1500. The sleeping guards around Christ's tomb have several items of Moorish arms, armour and costume, but still look very different from their North African co-religionists. (Museo Diocesana, Barcelona)

BELOW LEFT **A portrait of Queen Isabel of Castile in a panel painting attributed to Juan de Flandes. (Prado, Madrid)**

BELOW RIGHT **King Fernando II of Aragon, in an anonymous panel painting almost certainly made during his lifetime. (Staatliche Museen Preussischer Kulturbesitz, Berlin)**

THE ROYAL FAMILIES OF ARAGON AND CASTILE

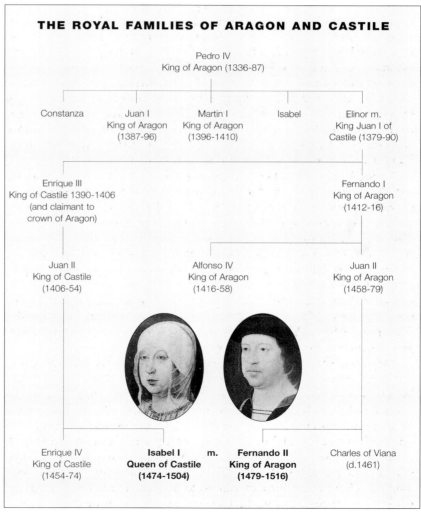

Pedro IV
King of Aragon (1336-87)

Constanza — Juan I King of Aragon (1387-96) — Martin I King of Aragon (1396-1410) — Isabel — Elinor m. King Juan I of Castile (1379-90)

Enrique III King of Castile 1390-1406 (and claimant to crown of Aragon) — Fernando I King of Aragon (1412-16)

Juan II King of Castile (1406-54) — Alfonso IV King of Aragon (1416-58) — Juan II King of Aragon (1458-79)

Enrique IV King of Castile (1454-74) — **Isabel I Queen of Castile (1474-1504)** m. **Fernando II King of Aragon (1479-1516)** — Charles of Viana (d.1461)

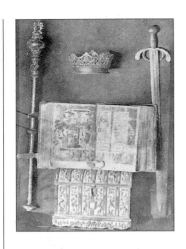

The sceptre, crown, sword, Psalter and chest said to have belonged to Queen Isabel of Aragon. (Cathedral Treasury, Granada)

Seville, but this declined in the 1480s, perhaps because he saw which way the religious wind was blowing and, being partly of *converso* origin himself, he could not feel entirely safe from the 'purity of blood' ideas then spreading across Spain. Perhaps it was a sense of self-preservation which made De Guzman one of the most enthusiastic commanders in the war which destroyed Granada.

Don Diégo Fernández de Cordoba, Count of Cabra, was the first man to hold that title. He was also Marshal of Castile and one of the most senior military commanders in Spain. Born at Baena in 1438, Don Diégo Fernández was still a very young man when he first served in the army of King Enrique IV. He was made Count of Cabra in 1458, but only became one of the most famous warriors in Spain under the leadership of King Fernando. It was, however, his capture of Muhammad XII 'Boabdil' which caught the Spanish imagination, as a traditional Andalusian song said:

> On the wall of Baena, his hand in his beard,
> Resting on his chest, the Little King wept,
> On how he had been imprisoned,
> Despite his courage, by he of Cabra.

RIGHT **The full armour of King Fernando, made in northern Italy but incorporating several Spanish features such as a 'fish-tail' plackart. (Inv. A.5, affensammlung, Kunsthistorisches Museum, Vienna)**

LEFT **The ceremonial sword and scabbard of** *Los Reyes Catolicos* **which was later used by the Habsburg Emperors. (Inv. G.1 and G.2, Real Armeria, Madrid)**

BELOW **One of the two war swords of King Fernando of Aragon. This magnificent late 15th century weapon is in an Iberian-Islamic tradition associated with light cavalry combat** *a la jinete*. **(Inv. G.31, Real Armeria, Madrid).**

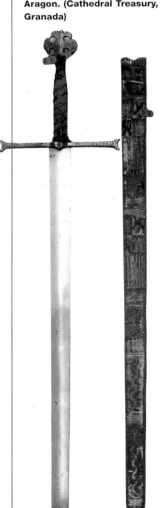

MOORISH LEADERS

Muhammad XII's Spanish name, 'Boabdil', was a corruption of his Arabic name, Abû 'Abd 'Allah. He became rival Amir or ruler in 1482 when he rebelled against his father Abû'l-Hassan 'Alî. Muhammad XII soon felt it necessary to achieve a military success to legitimise his position, but the result was his defeat near Lucena and the first of several imprisonments at the hands of Fernando and Isabel. At the same time Muhammad XII was supported by the Granadan political faction which hoped for peace with the Spaniards. Muhammad XII himself was brave but inexperienced, and only 19 or 20 years old when he came to the throne. Easily swayed by the advice of counsellors, his formidable mother and eventually by the people of Granada themselves, he ended up leading a doomed stand against the Spanish invaders – only to surrender in secret when the final confrontation came.

Family politics within the private quarters or *harîm* of the Alhambra palace remain obscure and have been complicated by legend. Muhammad XII's mother Fatima was the first wife of Amir Abû'l-Hassan 'Alî, and in Spanish mythology she is said to have been a bitter rival of the Amir's concubine Zurayda, herself a Spanish slave girl originally named Isabel de Solis. Fatima (also called Aisha in these stories) was portrayed as the scheming and ruthless counterpart of the saintly Queen Isabel of Castile. In reality Fatima and the real-life Aisha both appear to have been daughters of Muhammad X, a previous Amir of Granada, while Fatima's marriage to Amir Abû'l-Hassan 'Alî was dynastic and

Part of a wall painting based on a lost early 16th century tapestry illustrating the battle of Higueruela. It shows the walled city of Granada and the surrounding fertile *vega* as they would have appeared during the final siege. (Sala de Batallas, Escorial Monastery).

THE NASRID DYNASTY OF GRANADA

The use of numbers to identify Muslim rulers was only found in Spanish sources and was not used by Arabic chroniclers.

Muhammad V
Amir (1354-59 and 1362-91)

Yûsuf II
Amir (1391-92

Nasr

'Alî

Yûsuf III
Amir
(1408-17)

Ahmad

Muhammad VII
Amir
(1392-1408)

Muhammad IX 'Uthmân
Amir
(1419-27, 1430-31)

Yûsuf V
Amir (1445/6-62)

Muhammad X
Amir (1445-47)

Muhammad VIII
Amir (1417-19 and 1427-29)

Muhammad XI Amir (1448-54)

Outside this family tree:
Yûsuf, Amir (1431-32;
1432-45 and 1447-53)

Sa'ad
Amir
(1454-62 and 1462-64)

Muhammad XIII al-Zagal
(Rival Amir during reign
Muhammad XII 'Boabdil')

Abû'l-Hassan 'Alî   m.   Fâtima
Amir   (1st wife)
(1464-85)

RIGHT **Anonymous panel painting of Muhammad XII, better known as 'Boabdil, King of Granada'. Unlike most other supposed portraits of the last Amir of Granada, this probably shows him as he really looked. (Location unknown)**

Muhammad XII 'Boabdil'
(1482-91)

resulted in two sons (including Muhammad 'Boabdil') and a daughter also named Aisha. The real Zurayya was the Amir Abû'l-Hassan 'Alî's second wife, who bore him two further sons.

Muhammad XIII, known as al-Zagal, never caught the popular imagination in the way the tragic young Amir Muhammad XII 'Boabdil' did. He was the old Amir Abû'l-Hassan 'Alî's brother and thus Muhammad XII's uncle. The disastrous political split between these men, called a *fitna* in Arabic sources, was largely blamed for the ruin of the Amirate. In 1483 most Muslim legal authorities in Granada issued a *fatwa* or judgement denying Muhammad XII 'Boabdil's' right to rule because of his perceived friendship with Castile. For the next two years al-Zagal led the anti-Boabdil forces within the Amirate until, early in 1485, the old Amir Abû'l-Hassan 'Alî suffered a stroke and, unable to rule, was replaced by his brother al-Zagal who became known as Muhammad XIII. Nevertheless, Granada remained divided – much to the advantage of its Christian foes. It was during these turbulent years that Muhammad XIII earned his title of al-Zagal, or 'the Valorous', winning the support of many military and political leaders unhappy with Muhammad XII 'Boabdil's' vacillating leadership. In the end he also came to realise that defeat was inevitable and made his peace but, unable to endure the humiliation, he left for what is now Algeria where he died in circumstances which are lost in legend.

Hamîd al-Zagrî was probably part of the political faction which urged a struggle to the finish. Even his name remains slightly uncertain, some sources calling him Hamete Zeli, others Ahmad al-Thagrî, or 'the Frontiersman'. Very little is known about him except that he was described as a 'doughty old warrior', was a loyal supporter of Muhammad XIII al-Zagal,

The crimson *Marlûta* or coat of Muhammad XII with his turban-cloth rolled up on a bar above the coat. (Museo del Ejército, Madrid)

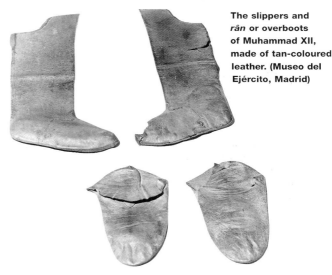

The slippers and *rân* or overboots of Muhammad XII, made of tan-coloured leather. (Museo del Ejército, Madrid)

TOP LEFT **Helmet also said to have been taken from Muhammad XII. (Metropolitan Museum of Art, New York)**

LEFT **Dagger of the type known as an 'ear dagger', its sheath, an eating knife, a small pouch and a belt with a larger pouch taken from Muhammad XII during his first captivity. (Inv. G.361, Real Armeria, Madrid)**

an opponent of Muhammad XII 'Boabdil', and commanded a small garrison of North African volunteers in Ronda and Malaga. After the fall of Malaga, Hamîd al-Zagrî was imprisoned in Carmona, and nothing further is known of his fate, though he might have been among those prisoners said to have been formed into a slave-guard for the Pope in Rome.

Ibrahîm 'Alî al-'Attâr was another very old, but obscure, warrior. He rose from a common soldier to high military command and was particularly experienced in frontier skirmishing. The fact that Muhammad XII 'Boabdil' married 'Alî al-'Attâr's daughter indicates that the old soldier had also acquired political as well as military influence. He defended Loja against attack by King Fernando in 1482 but was killed during Muhammad XII's raid around Lucena the following year, being then in his late eighties.

OPPOSING FORCES

SPANISH ARMIES

Although Castile had far greater resources than Granada, it was the southern provinces of Andalusia which served as the main arsenal, granary and base for its armies. Payment in Spanish armies was also higher than in Italy or France, reflecting a lingering Islamic tradition, but even so, Spanish soldiers received less than their Moorish opponents. The Spanish artillery formed an élite, and Isabel recruited gunners from France, Germany and Italy, as well as other Spanish kingdoms, all commanded by an engineer named Francisco Ramírez. Some of the great guns had a crew of 200 men though only a handful were fully trained gunners. While the artillery formed a technological élite, the old aristocratic cavalry remained the most prestigious part of the army. These included knights who were direct vassals of the crown and those who owed service to the grandees of Spain who still had considerable military power.

The 15th century Castilian fortress of Alcala la Real which towered over the neighbouring Granadan frontier. (Author's photograph)

The 15th century Spanish aristocratic élite were expected to be good judges of military equipment and to take part in various forms of tournament. These included ordinary *torneos* with armoured jousting and foot combat, as well as typically Andalusian light cavalry *jinete* (games) called *Juegos de Cañas* using light spears or javelins. Training also included a form of mounted bullfight. Men from all sections of society seemed eager to fight the Moors, who were regarded as such good fighting men that they could only be defeated with God's help. For most men with a claim to noble status, fear of *vergüenza*, or the 'shame' that could be brought to one's family or lineage, similarly inspired courage and loyalty.

The bulk of the ordinary infantry came from all over Castile via the *Hermandad* system of urban leagues. Additional infantry were recruited and organised by royal *continos*, or agents, and unemployed labourers formed a large part of the volunteers. Others were *homicianos*, or criminals, who were offered a pardon in return for military service. The bulk

Two high relief carvings on the Triumphal Arch of King Alfonso, made around 1470. The soldiers probably include southern Italians and Aragonese, since Naples was then under the Aragonese crown. (*In situ*, Castel Nuovo, Naples)

of militias involved in the conquest of Granada came from Andalusian *Hermandadas*, and included cavalry, mounted crossbowmen and around five times as many foot soldiers. They were summoned from specified areas known as *Adelantamientos* and fought in the units in which they were recruited. Experts in frontier warfare came from closer to the border, and were known as *almogávares*, or *adalides*. Several local grandees such as Rodrigo Ponce de León, the Marquis of Cadiz, also had their own highly effective intelligence networks. The *Santa Hermandad* was a separate system, almost a form of royal conscription established in 1476, in which all registered urban tax-payers had to pay a contribution or serve in the ranks. Yet even the *Santa Hermandad* suffered from the non-appearance of its pay. As a result written promissory notes were given and then circulated like paper money.

Mudejars, or Muslims living under Christian rule, played a significant role in the non-combatant transport services as smiths, armourers or veterinary experts. Some Spanish noblemen also employed Moorish drummers and flute-players, but most of the Moors who fought for Castile and Aragon were temporary 'allies' from Granada's fractured political factions. Perhaps the most unexpected members of the Castilian army during these years were Guanches or natives of the Canary Islands, including a few soldiers of Guanche origin who were present in the final siege of Granada.

Aragon's military contribution to the conquest of Granada was less

A detail from the funerary monument of the Infante Alfonso, brother of the future Queen Isabel, by Gil de Siloe, 1489-93. This man-at-arms is equipped for combat on foot. (*In situ* the Cartuja de Miraflores, Burgos)

than was once thought and the Aragonese nobility only took part in large numbers from 1487 onwards. An important part of the Aragonese king's own forces included mercenaries. Aragonese urban militias felt no social or military inferiority to the knightly aristocracy, while beyond the cities there was another form of rural militia called the *sometent*. The Aragonese crown also employed troops from Sicily. During the conquest of Granada the role of foreign volunteers was important for religious and propaganda reasons, though their numbers remained small. One of the most exotic – from the Spanish point of view – was Lord Scales from England. Others included English archers and axemen, Swiss infantry, Burgundian gunners and artillerymen sent by the Emperor Maximilian.

A crossbow, probably dating from the early 16th rather than late 15th century. This simple but powerful weapon was made for war rather than hunting. (Museo del Ejército, Madrid)

Castilian armies were changing rapidly in the late 15th century, but they remained very mixed forces in terms of organisation. The artillery was the only autonomous unit within what might be called the 'royal army'. The army itself was nevertheless quite impressive, consisting of an artillery train; heavy cavalry men-at-arms organised into *lanzas*, or small fighting units; around ten times as many light cavalry *jinetes*; and assorted types of infantry. Contrary to what was once thought, there was no *Guardas Reales*, or royal guard, during the war for Granada, as this was not created until 1493. Instead Fernando and Isabel had armed escorts of courtiers.

The feudal retinues of the higher Spanish nobility consisted of the same sorts of troops, though generally without artillery and with a larger proportion of cavalry. The Church also provided comparable forces led by several warrior bishops. Although their importance had declined, the Military Orders of Santiago, Calatrava and Alcantara still provided well trained and highly-motivated contingents. At the start of the war for Granada these assorted non-royal forces numbered around 4,700 cavalry, but only 3,400 infantry. By 1489, however, the higher nobility alone could field 7,461 horsemen and 5,795 foot soldiers, while the city militias furnished another 1,900 cavalry and no fewer than 12,800 infantry. The border with Granada had its own separate military organisation, with Cadiz, Seville, Cordoba, Jaen and Cazorla serving as base areas, while numerous fortresses stood closer to the frontier itself.

On campaign the organisation of Spanish armies was fluid and mixed, although the mustering of men, their lodgings along the proposed route and their organisation into *capitanías* – units – were all decided beforehand. On campaign Castilian forces were divided into *battles* for tactical purposes, perhaps reflecting the units of 50 men under a captain described in the mid-15th century *Tirant lo Blanc*. Heavy cav-

Detail from a painting of *The Death of St Peter Martyr* by Pedro Berruguete, late 15th century, illustrating the crossbow equipment of the period. (Inv. LVII no. 613, Prado, Madrid)

The *Retablo de San Miguel* by Maestro de Cervera, 1450-1500. Here St George is shown in a fancifully decorated version of 15th century armour. (Museo Episcopal, Vic)

alry, *lanzas-hombre de armas*, consisting of the man-at-arms, his more lightly armoured squire, page, servant and two mounted crossbowmen, may have been largely administrative, while in battle the knight seems to have fought alone or with his squire in support. The *lanzas a la jinete* consisted of squadrons of light cavalry. The infantry were organised along medieval lines, insofar as they were organised at all.

One of the biggest problems faced by Castilian armies operating inside Granadan territory was feeding their men. Not only had the local Moorish population usually fled, taking available food resources with them, but the Spanish tactic of devastation soon led to their own hunger. Consequently, convoys carried wheat to the army in the field, which was then sold to the soldiers at half its normal price. In the campaign of 1482–3, for example, 80,000 mules were needed to deliver such food.

The strategy and tactics used by late 15th century Spanish armies owed a great deal to medieval traditions, which in turn reflected close contacts with the Muslim world. Siege warfare was paramount. Raiding economic targets such as crops, orchards and mills was considered the best way to undermine the enemy's ability to resist, while a field army needed plenty of crossbowmen to resist enemy cavalry. Strong defensive positions were also essential on the march because the Moors were more mobile and adept at sudden ambushes. More recently, however, western European tactical ideas had taken hold. Consequently a *batalla* or 'battle' often consisted of ten *cuadrilla* or squadrons each of around 50 men and led by a *cuadrillero*. Ideally, five *batallas* were considered a division, though in reality such divisions had no standard size or structure. One thing is, however, clear: there was a gradual reduction in the number and importance of fully armoured cavalrymen during the war for Granada, and a corresponding increase in other arms, especially the artillery. The downside of this development was that surprise was now virtually impossible, as roads had to be cleared well ahead of an army so that the heavy artillery could move.

The traditional strategy of raiding and ravaging continued, though this was dominated by the need to use relatively few *puertos* or passes through the rugged Sierra mountains around the Amirate of Granada.

The Bearing of the Cross by the German artist Martin Schongauer. The same cavalryman wearing a helmet and half-cuirass covered in decorative cloth and rivets is here shown from the rear, whereas in the print of *The Battle of Clavijo*, he is shown from the front.
(Musée de Colmar)

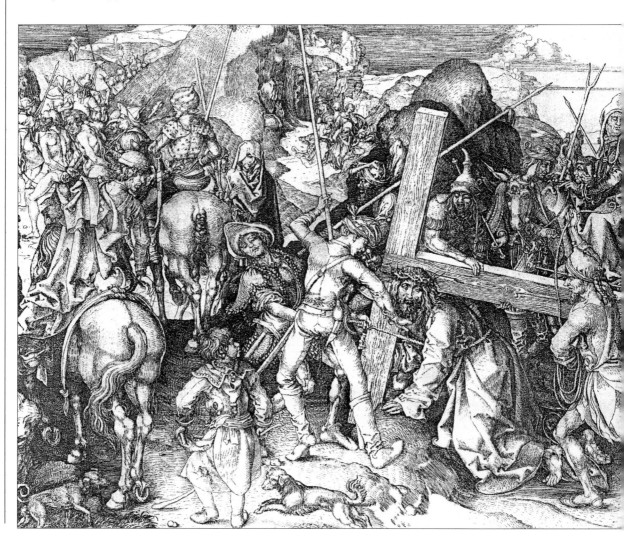

The country outside Medina Sidonia. This broad landscape lent itself to the rustling which characterised 15th century border warfare between Castile and Granada. (Author's photograph)

In such warfare both sides used sophisticated early warning systems with hilltop observation towers and beacons to give the inhabitants time to move themselves and their livestock out of harm's way. The troops engaged in such warfare also fought in relatively open order, skirmishing, ambushing and moving remarkably quickly across the rugged terrain. Armoured cavalry had, however, been decisive in the great battles of the Reconquista and the armies of northern Castile still thought in this way. Senior commanders still had great faith in the impact of heavily armoured horsemen on enemy morale, though the war for Granada showed that such troops rarely hit their intended targets. Consequently, light cavalry *a la jinete* increased in numbers. Their tactics had become something of a sport in southern Spain, with the game of *juege de cañas* being played by teams of horsemen armed with light reed spears and leather shields.

The Iberian peninsula was one of several parts of 15th century Europe famous for their infantry. Tactically, they had much in common with those of 15th century Italy, emphasising the offensive use of light infantry operating out of strong field fortifications in close co-operation with cavalry. Their own confidence against enemy horsemen is summed up in the early 16th century Spanish saying; *'Muerto el caballo, perdito el hombre d'armas' (When the horse is dead, the man-at-arms is lost).'* In fact, Spanish armies placed great emphasis on field fortifications, particularly when facing a highly manoeuvrable Moorish foe. The Spanish were also skilled at using field fortifications to secure a bridgehead following a naval landing, and had perfected this by the time the Conquistadores invaded America.

Spanish siege warfare was traditional, except in its use of increasing numbers of heavy cannon. The most famous siege device during the conquest of Granada was the 'counter-city' of Santa Fé, built as a permanent base during the final attack on the city of Granada. Yet this was not a new idea, having been a feature of Moorish Andalusian and North African siege warfare for several centuries. The treatment of conquered Muslim peoples varied greatly. The rural population was usually allowed

The magnificent sword, scabbard
and incomplete baldric of
Muhammad XII, the last Amir
of Granada.
(Museo del
Ejército, Madrid)

to remain as tax-paying *mudejars* under royal protection, but urban populations were almost always expelled, although in some cases they were permitted to move into the surrounding countryside or suburbs.

For centuries Castile had been technologically rather isolated from the rest of western Europe (though this was changing by the late 15th century), while Aragon had been more outward looking. As a result the arms and armour of their military élites were virtually identical, while that of humbler Castilian warriors preserved several archaic features. Christian light cavalry fighting *a la jinete* also had many features in common with their Moorish rivals, including lighter armour, a shorter spear which could be thrown as a javelin, a light slashing sword or large dagger, a distinctive kidney-shaped leather *adarga* shield, and a low saddle with broad stirrups and relatively short stirrup-leathers. Some of these horsemen were also armed with crossbows.

There was widespread belief in miracle-working swords on the Christian side of the frontier, the most famous weapon being the Sword of St Ferdinand (King Ferdinand III) which was kept in Seville Cathedral. The sword represented three things to the Spanish military élite: strength, justice and the Christian Cross. The mace revived in popularity in Christian Iberia in the 15th century, yet the hero in *Tirant lo Blanc* still maintained that the horseman's axe of Islamic origin remained the deadliest weapon when fighting in full armour, when it was hung from a cavalryman's saddle-bow. By now the crossbow, in its heavier infantry form, was an extremely powerful weapon with a pull of up to 300kg, great power-to-weight ratio and astonishing accuracy. Stirrups and belt hooks were generally used to span the lighter forms of crossbow, particularly on horseback, while pulleys were needed for heavier types.

Cannon had appeared in southern Castile before they reached the north but the acceptance of firearms was generally slower in Castile than in neighbouring Aragon. The Moors of Granada were undoubtedly quicker to use firearms, though by the late 15th century their Christian opponents had overtaken them. The huge cannon preferred in earlier years were being phased out in favour of a larger number of smaller, standardised guns, while cannon-balls ranged from 500g to 50kg, the biggest guns having a range of around 2,000m, though it was only possible to fire these once an hour. By the 1480s handguns with long barrels to increase muzzle velocity were being made in both Cordoba and Ecija under the guidance of French masters, and some of these may have been early forms of matchlock with a serpentine or pivoted piece of metal to hold the match.

MOORISH ARMIES

Local troops continued to dominate the Granadan army until the fall of the Amirate in 1492. The majority were recruited in a traditional manner through the *Diwân al-Jaysh*, or army ministry, salaries being paid according to rank. In addition there were always a certain number of religiously motivated *ghuzât*, volunteers from North Africa. So many originated from the Zanâta tribe that they gave their name to a characteristic style of light cavalry warfare, *a la jinete*.

The size of the army varied; an Egyptian visitor in 1465 maintained that Granada had 80,000 archers, though this was exaggerated. A review in 1478 involved 4,700 garrison cavalry. The lowest Christian estimate put the army of the Amirate at 3,000 cavalry and 50,000 infantry, while a major raid in 1483 involved between 1,200 and 1,500 horsemen. The bulk of Granadan soldiers and part-time militiamen were infantry, while the army also included doctors, labourers, armourers and clerks.

More obviously part of the Granadan military élite was the Amir's guard of *mamlûks*, also known as *ma'lûghûn*. Recruited from young Christian prisoners converted to Islam, they were educated in the Alhambra palace. They were regarded as *renegados* – traitors – by the Christians, and tended to receive short shrift if captured. Unlike the *mamlûks* of Egypt, however, these men could expect their own sons to reach senior military positions. Ordinary militias came from towns and rural areas, the high Alpujarra valleys south-east of Granada being famous for their skilled infantry crossbowmen. *Thagrî* frontiersmen also formed a distinct group under their own leaders.

The motivation of Granada's military personnel was a mixture of traditional religious commitment and enthusiasm for defensive *jihâd*, plus a personal honour code that had much in common with the chivalry seen on the Spanish side of the frontier.

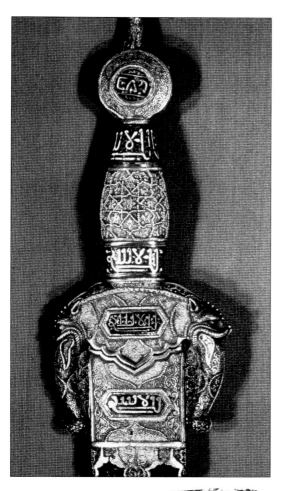

ABOVE **One of the most highly decorated 15th century swords of the so-called Granadan style. (Cabinet des Medailles, Bibliothèque Nationale, Paris**

RIGHT **A different sort of short-sword or long dagger said to have belonged to Muhammad XII. (Museo del Ejército, Madrid)**

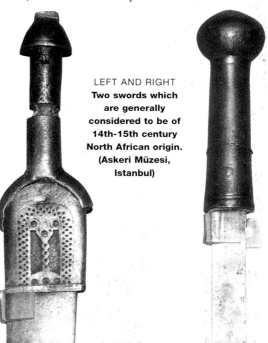

LEFT AND RIGHT **Two swords which are generally considered to be of 14th-15th century North African origin. (Askeri Müzesi, Istanbul)**

31

Granadan armies had always been accompanied by the *sûfis* and other Muslim ascetics who inhabited frontier *ribâts* and took part in frontier raids, but as the final crisis came closer religious motivation became stronger. North African *ghuzzât* volunteers included those who settled Granada and dedicated their lives to the *jihâd*. All retained a strong North African identity and were not always popular with the local Granadan Moors.

The local Andalusian Moorish part of the Granadan army was commanded by a senior officer known as the *wâlî* who was often a close relative of the Amir, although on important campaigns the ruler frequently led the army in person. North African volunteer *ghuzzât* were commanded by their own *shaykh* who was again usually related either to the Amir or the Sultan of Fez. The permanent professional core of the army largely consisted of cavalry based in fortress garrisons, the largest of these being in Granada, Malaga, Ronda and Guadix. In addition there were 30 administrative or military regions, 13 having large fortresses.

In fact, the Amirate of Granada was very strongly fortified with most cities having been enlarged to accommodate the influx of refugees. The most important fortress was the Alcazaba at one end of the Alhambra palace overlooking Granada city which, in the late 15th century, had been given three massive semi-circular artillery bastions. Elsewhere most fortifications continued to rely on the height and strength of their walls – defences which would fail when the Spaniards brought up their powerful new guns.

Granadan tactical organisation was based on established Islamic military traditions dating back to the 9th century if not earlier. The structure of command and control was far clearer, and thus presumably more effective, than in neighbouring Spanish armies. Nasrid military banners and court vestments were red, and the army made considerable use of drums and fifes to maintain morale. Granadan troops also wore some sort of distinctive emblem. According to the Catalan author of *Tirant lo Blanc*, the Muslims identified their dead with pieces of leather bearing the deceased's name, though this could also be interpreted as a very early form of 'dog-tag' worn by each soldier.

Moorish strategy reflected their limited resources: it was essentially defensive, and governed by the geographical situation in a small mountainous corner of Iberia, cut off by sea from the rest of the Muslim world. Consequently raids to punish or deter enemy attacks were balanced by harassment and ambush tactics when Granada's territory was invaded. On those few occasions when Moorish forces confronted the Spaniards in open battle, Granadan tactics were extremely traditional and less effective than they had proved in earlier centuries. Infantry still adopted a strong defensive position, while cavalry mounted repeated but relatively small charges to wear down and break the enemy. Moorish cavalry tactics themselves were both more distinctive and more effective. Though essentially the same as those used by Muslim armies in the Middle East, the Moors used javelins and crossbows rather than Turkish-style hand-held bows.

Undecorated 15th-16th century adarga leather shield. (Royal Armouries, Leeds)

The Arab and Berber tradition of archery was an infantry affair, and in Granada this had evolved into a sophisticated tradition of crossbow warfare. When writing about crossbows at the end of the 14th century, Ibn Hudhayl maintained that, *'All the art and all the mystery rests on the way on which the trigger is squeezed. This squeezing can be done in three ways. Men well versed in the art do it softly, those less good do it bit by bit'.* Other Granadan infantry, perhaps including the less professional members of the militias, were armed with ordinary hand-bows, swords, daggers, long spears, slings, kidney-shaped leather shields and rectangular mantlets. By the late 15th century many also had handguns.

Berber North African influence on the arms, armour, costume and tactics of later 15th century Granada was less than is sometimes thought. For example, although the Granadan élite wore less armour than its Castilian foes, it also used more than its North African allies, particularly in its adoption of a Spanish-style open-faced *salet* helmet and scale-lined brigandines. Although much war gear was captured from the enemy, Moorish craftsmen were still making weapons in the Albaicin quarter of Granada; the last craftsmen or their descendants were still active in North Africa in the early 16th century. Granadan crossbows included several different types, ranging from a light form used on horseback, to massive weapons used in siege warfare. In fact Ibn Hudhayl described these weapons as *'one of the marvels of human industry'.*

This extraordinary crossbow was found in the village of Mécina Bombarón in the Alpujarras Valley and dates from the 15th century. (Museo Arqueológico, Granada)

Other Moorish weapons included slings, which reflected the existence of a substantial animal herding population, and the large *azegaya* cavalry javelin which may have originated south of the Sahara. Some of these had special armour-piercing heads. A form of short slightly curved sabre also reached Morocco and Granada by the late 15th century while the slender thrusting dagger had been regarded as a typically Berber weapon since at least the 11th century. The kidney-shaped leather *daraqa* shield known to the Spanish as the *adarga* was, however, the most distinctive piece of Moorish military equipment and was probably a development of the larger *lamt* leather shields of medieval times. Very little information survives about the small amount of armour worn in Granada. Only a small minority of 15th century Granadan troops wore metallic armour, though these were not necessarily senior men. Crossbowmen, for example, sometimes wore helmets and light body armour, whereas hand gunners did not.

Cannon were probably used by Granadan forces at the siege of Huescar in 1324 and there is no doubt about their use in defence of Algeciras 19 years later. It also appears that Muslim troops from Granada were the first to use handguns in Iberia at the battle of Egea in 1394, but from the mid-15th century onwards virtually all Granadan firearms were probably captured from the Christians.

OPPOSING PLANS

CASTILIAN INVASION PLANS

Two details from a late 15th century tapestry illustrating the Portuguese seizure of Arzila and Tangier in 1471. The commander with the fabric-covered helmet and staff of office is King Alfonso V, called 'Africanus'. (Museo Parroquial, Pastrana, prov. of Guadalajara)

The conquest of Granada was not only one of the most intensive campaigns of the 15th century, but was also in many ways a new Renaissance-style war involving a high degree of ruthlessness. In strategic terms King Fernando planned to roll up the Amirate like a carpet, starting at the edges and finishing with the city of Granada. Another analogy used by Fernando and Queen Isabel was that of the pomegranate fruit which was the symbol of Granada. When he vowed to pick out the pomegranate's seeds one by one, Fernando meant that he would take the fortified castles and towns one at a time. To enable his armies to take these positions, however, Fernando's troops had to reduce the Granadan ability to resist by devastating their agricultural surroundings. This involved *tala* or the destruction of crops, orchards, irrigation systems, mills and other agricultural facilities on a scale not attempted before. It was so successful that the Muslim peasantry were forced to leave their farms and villages and flee to the fortified centres, thus increasing pressure on the limited food supplies in these towns and castles. This strategy also denied Moorish troops food and a friendly population amongst whom to operate while harassing the invaders. Furthermore, the Moors could not afford to lose the food and other supplies in fortified bases and were thus obliged to defend even those they may otherwise have abandoned. *Tala* or devastation was generally carried out by feudal forces commanded by the Spanish nobility, while the main sieges were left to the more modern

The hill facing the citadel of Vélez Malaga where King Fernando was almost captured during the Spanish siege of that town. The Mediterranean can be seen in the distance. (Author's photograph)

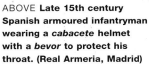

ABOVE **Late 15th century Spanish armoured infantryman wearing a *cabacete* helmet with a *bevor* to protect his throat. (Real Armeria, Madrid)**

RIGHT **Late 15th century Spanish man-at-arms with a straight-bladed pole-axe. (Musée de l'Armée, Paris)**

TOP RIGHT **Late 15th century Spanish crossbowman wearing a scale-lined brigandine and using a windlass to span his weapon. (Real Armeria, Madrid)**

royal armies, usually commanded by King Fernando in person. Meanwhile, the Castilian and Aragonese fleets attempted to blockade Granada's coast, at least during the summer when the seas were traditionally regarded as being 'open' for navigation.

GRANADA'S DEFENCE PLANS

Granada's options were far more limited, and the Amirate was also weakened by internal political dissension. There was also no real help from the rest of the Muslim world because of the chaotic situation among former allies in North Africa, and the distance of both Mamlûk Egypt and the Ottoman Turkish Empire from the scene of war. The armies of Granada were also in a weak tactical position, as the western part of their heavily fortified frontier zone had already been pushed back a long way. The most vulnerable frontiers were in the west, where the mountains were pierced by fertile river valleys which formed *puertos* (passes) into the heartlands of the Amirate.

Fundamentally, however, repeated Spanish attacks with an efficient artillery train and large siege cannon spelled Granada's doom. The size of the invading forces also enabled the Spanish to withstand Granada's harassment tactics. Since the armies of Granada were unable to drive the Spanish invaders away, or to defeat them in open battle, their only real answer would have been to retreat into the mountains and conduct a guerrilla war. But this would have meant abandoning the cities which were the cultural centre of Andalusian Islamic civilisation – an unthinkable option until it was too late.

'Chosroes' envoy delivering a message to the Satrap', in the early 16th century *Sulwân al-Mutâ'* made in Granada after the fall of the Moorish state, but before the expulsion of the Muslim population. (Ms. 528, Library, Escorial Monastery

A battle between rival Moorish armies on a century panel painting attributed to Gherardo Stanina or the Maestro dei Bambino Vispo, c.1425. It shows North African military costume and light cavalry combat *a la jinete*. (Staatliches Lindenau-Museum, Altenburg)

EVENTS 1481-1485

Granadan raids & defensive movements:

1 Early in 1482 Moorish troops from Ronda raid the Arcos area.

2 Abû'l-Hasan's army marches from Granada in an attempt to retake Alhama; unsuccessfully beseiges the castle from 5th to 19th March 1482 then returns to Granada.

3 Mid-July 1482 Abû'l-Hasan reached Loja from Granada and sweeps the country around the Rio Frio.

4 Al-Zagal's garrison in Malaga marches out to face the raiders in late March 1483, the Moorish cavalry operating in the valleys while the infantry control the hills. They attack the Spanish rearguard then defeat the entire force.

5 Abû ᶜAbdullah leads his men from Loja to beseige Lucena and ravage as far as Aguillar. The appearance of a Spanish relief force obliges Abû ᶜAbdullah to retreat on 20th April, but he is defeated and captured near Fuentes de Cesna on 21st April 1483. Abû ᶜAbdullah is subsequently released in the hope of dividing Moorish loyalties in the Emirate of Granada.

6 Al-Zagal's troops in Malaga march to join the garrison of Ronda in a large raid towards Utrera early in September 1483. The infantry are left to guard the pass homeward and a cavalry ambush is established on the river Lopera, the rest of the cavalry raiding the Utrera area where they are attacked and forced to retreat to the river Lopera. The larger part of the Moorish raiding force reassembles near the river Guadalete but is defeated by Spanish troops from Jerez and retreats into the Sierra de Ronda, towards the awaiting ambush party. The Moorish cavalry try to attack the Spanish rear while the Spanish attack the Moorish infantry defending the pass, but both parts of the Moorish army are defeated. The smaller part of the Moorish cavalry force breaks off combat and makes its way home in a wide sweep through Spanish territory past Lebrixa and Arcos then back to Ronda through the Sierra de Ronda.

7 February 1485, Al-Zagal drives Abû ᶜAbdullah from Almeria; Abû ᶜAbdullah flees to King Fernando in Cordoba. He is later returned to Granada with Spanish help.

8 Al-Zagal's army assembles in Ronda and attempts unsuccessfully to relieve Coin and Cartama in April 1485.

9 Early-mid-May 1485, the garrison of Ronda raids the area around Medina Sidonia but returns to find Ronda itself beseiged by King Fernando.

10 Late May 1486, Al-Zagal marches from Malaga to Granada to take over as Emir following his brother Abû'l-Hasan's heart attack; defeats a foraging party from Alhama on the way.

11 Early September 1485, Al-Zagal leads his troops from Granada to support Moclin; defeats part of the invading Spanish army and enters Moclin.

Spanish raids, invasions & defensive movements:

1 Spanish forces gather at Marchena, march to Antequera, cross the Sierra Alzerifa and seize Alhama from the north on 28th February 1482.

2 King Fernando marches to Lucena in support of Alhama, sends reinforcements which reach Alhama on 30th April 1482, himself returning to Cordoba to take command of a larger force. Fernando takes official possession of Alhama on 14th May 1482.

3 King Fernando and his army cross the river Genil at Ecija, reach Loja on 1st July, are defeated by the garrison under ᶜAlí al-ᶜAṭṭár and withdraw to Cordoba.

4 The Castillian fleet is sent to patrol the Straits and prevent reinforcements reaching Granada from Morocco.

5 Spanish force leaves Antequera on 19th March 1483, marches through Ajarquía mountains towards Malaga, intending to return home via the coast. Some cavalry reaches the walls of Malaga, but then the army retreats back into the mountains, becomes lost and is defeated in late March. Survivors scatter to Antequera, Alhama and elsewhere.

6 Fernando's army ravages the areas of Illora (8th April 1483) & Tajár (14th April 1483); resupplies the Spanish garrison at Alhama (16th April 1483).

7 Mid-April 1483, the Count of Cabra leads the Spanish forces in Baena across the sierras towards Lucena; attacks Abû ᶜAbdullah (Boabdil) from the Sierra de la Horconera, defeat and capture him near Fuentes de Cesna on 21st April 1483.

8 Spanish garrisons at Ecija, Utrera and elsewhere are alerted. Many assemble near Jerez; pursue and defeat part of the Moorish raiding force near Lopera on 17th September 1483; go on to retake Zahara in October.

9 Spanish army assembles at Antequera in spring 1484, and is led by King Fernando to Alora; raids the areas of Coin, Cazarabonela, Almejia, Cartama, Pupiana, Alhendrin and the Vega of Malaga. Is there resupplied by ships from Seville; returns via Coin, Allagagra, Gatero and Alhamin to Antequera.

10 Spanish capture Alora on 20th June 1484.

11 September 1484, Fernando sends the third raid of this year to the Vega of Granada; also leaving troops to support Abû ᶜAbdullah in Granada.

12 Spanish troops capture Senetil on 20th September 1484.

13 King Fernando leads his army out of Cordoba on 18th April 1485 to re-establish his authority in Benamaquex which had thrown off Spanish rule, then captures Coin (27th April 1485) and Cartama (28th April 1485). Fernando next leads part of this force to raid the Malaga area but is badly cut up by the garrison so turns to beseige Ronda on 8th May 1485. Ronda's water supply is cut off on 18th May and the city surrenders on 22nd May 1485.

14 King Fernando captures Casarabonela and Marbella on 15th June 1485.

15 Three groups of Spanish troops march from Alcala la Real to attack Moclin in late August 1485. The first group is ambushed by Al-Zagal in early September but is saved from rout by the second group. The third group under Fernando joins the others, and their target is changed from Moclin to the castles of Cambil and Albahar, both of which fall on 23rd September 1485.

16 In September 1485 the Spanish garrison in Alhama also seizes the castle of Zalea with the help of a traitor within the walls.

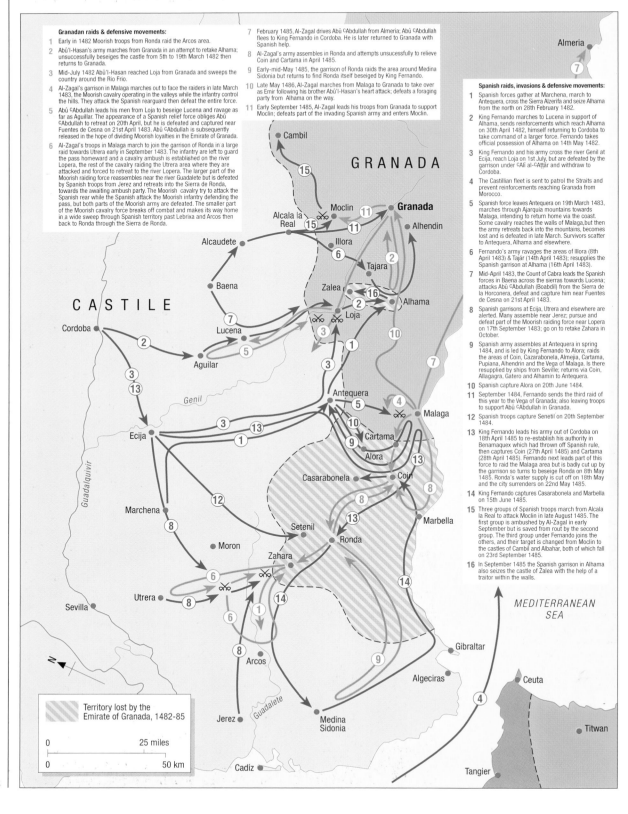

CASTILE

GRANADA

Almeria

Cambil

Moclin

Granada

Alcala la Real

Alhendin

Illora

Alcaudete

Tajara

Baena

Zalea

Alhama

Cordoba

Lucena

Loja

Aguilar

Genil

Antequera

Malaga

Ecija

Cartama

Alora

Casarabonela

Coin

Marchena

Marbella

Setenil

Moron

Ronda

Zahara

Guadalquivir

Gibraltar

Utrera

Algeciras

Ceuta

Sevilla

Arcos

MEDITERRANEAN SEA

Titwan

Jerez

Guadalete

Medina Sidonia

Cadíz

Tangier

Territory lost by the Emirate of Granada, 1482-85

0   25 miles

0   50 km

THE CAMPAIGN

ABOVE **Late 15th century Spanish man-at-arms equipped for light cavalry combat** *a la jinete*. **(Real Armeria, Madrid)**

RIGHT **Late 15th century Spanish man-at-arms equipped for heavy cavalry combat** *a la brida*. **(ex-Argaiz and Pauilhac Collections, present location unknown)**

The struggle for Granada went on for many years and largely consisted of raids and sieges without set-piece battles. Yet in this respect it was typical of many medieval and Renaissance campaigns. The purpose of this account is to explain what was, at least on the Spanish side, a carefully planned campaign which made full use of available resources, but which was nevertheless limited by difficult terrain, climate, inefficient technology and a highly tenacious foe.

The Truce of 1478 ended when troops of the Amir Abû'l-Hassan 'Alî seized the Castilian frontier town of Zahara as a reprisal for Spanish raids. It also followed the Amir's refusal to pay tribute. The attack on Zahara was itself a standard operation, catching the garrison by surprise on a stormy night on 26 December 1481, then taking the population away as captives.

Many in Granada, however, feared such a belligerent reply to Castilian demands, one aged *fâqi* (legal scholar) reputedly proclaiming; *'Woe to Granada! The hour of its desolation is at hand. The ruins of Zahara will fall upon our own heads.'* The fate of Zahara did provoke an even more successful counter-raid two months later by Rodrigo Ponce de León, Marquis of Cadiz. He learned that the strategic fortress of Alhama de Granada, deep inside the Amirate, was weakly garrisoned and so sent 2,500 cavalry and 3,000 infantry to seize it. For three nights the Spanish avoided densely populated valleys and approached over the wild Sierra Alzerifa to surprise the garrison before dawn on the rain-lashed winter night of 28 February 1482. Juan de Ortega, a captain of the élite escaladores, or 'climbers', and his men placed ladders against the fortress wall, slaughtered the garrison and threw open the gates for the marquis while the alarm was raised in the town below. A desperate struggle followed, but the invaders would not be dislodged.

King Fernando and Queen Isabel had not ordered this attack, though they would later claim credit for it, but Queen Isabel decided to use Alhama as a base for further conquests. Consequently, the taking of Alhama is regarded as the start of the final war for Granada. Its impact in Granada was just as great, since it was at the centre of the Muslim state and had been thought impregnable. Once again Spanish chroniclers recorded a quotation which may in fact have been heard in the streets of Granada: *'Woe for our Alhama! Alhama has fallen, the key to Granada is in the hands of the infidels.'*

Not surprisingly the Amir Abû'l-Hassan tried to regain Alhama in March, while also sending the garrison of Ronda to raid the home territory of the Duke of Cadiz around Arcos, but these efforts were in vain, and on 29 March Abû'l-Hassan returned to Granada when he learned that King Fernando himself was approaching. In fact the king remained at Lucena, having been advised not to hazard himself so deep inside enemy territory. So the Amir tried again to retake Alhama, but was not strong enough to do so. Fernando, meanwhile, assembled a larger force and took official possession of the fortress on 14 May.

During these months Queen Isabel was busy preparing Castile for a full-scale war which proved to be longer, more difficult and far more expensive than anticipated. Like most of his northern Spanish advisers, King Fernando failed to heed the advice of southern Spanish experts, one of whom was Diego de Valera who suggested that concentrating on taking the Amirate's main port of Malaga would lead to a speedier victory. Unfortunately De Valera, like so many Spanish intellectuals of that time, was of *converso* origin and thus his opinions were regarded with suspicion.

The Seizure of Alhama illustrated on one of the 54 carved wooden choir stalls commissioned by Cardinal Mendoza even before the end of the war for Granada. (*In situ*, Cathedral Choir, Toledo)

OVER-CONFIDENCE ON BOTH SIDES

Fernando and Isabel planned the first major expedition of the war against Loja, as an attempt to open up communications with the garrison at Alhama. The Amir Abû'l-Hassan knew a blow would fall soon and he urgently called for reinforcements from Morocco, but very few arrived. Castilian forces assembled before Loja under Fernando's command on 1 July 1482, and they too were fewer than expected. They included many soldiers from northern Spain who had no experience of fighting against the Moors. Nevertheless, Fernando wanted a quick triumph to bolster his prestige in Castile and so led them across the River Genil and camped amongst hills west of Loja. The terrain meant the Castilians were divided into several camps while the valley floor, which was cut up by irrigation canals, was unsuitable for the heavily armoured Castilian cavalry.

The commander of the *Hermandada* militias urged Fernando to cross the river downstream and approach Loja from the other side, but he was overruled by proud Castilian captains who similarly refused advice from more experienced Andalusian officers.

Instead, a large detachment under the Marquis of Cadiz, the Marquis of Villena and the Grand Master of Calatrava was sent to hold and fortify a steep hill known as the Heights of Albohacen, to be used as an artillery position dominating Loja. Before the Castilians could fortify these heights, 'Ali al-'Attâr the Moorish garrison commander sent a small force of light cavalry across the river during the night of 4–5 July. They hid, probably in woods on the eastern slope of the Heights of Albohacen, until the Christians on the summit, seeing 'Ali al-'Attâr's main force approaching from Loja, charged down the hillside. 'Ali al-'Attâr promptly retreated, drawing the Castilian cavalry after him, whereupon the concealed Muslim *jinetes* overran the partially completed fortifications on the hill and seized its artillery. The Castilian cavalry saw what was happening and turned back to defend their original position, so 'Ali al-'Attâr also turned and pursued them up the hill.

Fighting raged across the hilltop for an hour before a larger detachment of Castilians arrived and the Muslims withdrew into Loja. The Castilians suffered severely, and their dead included the youthful Rodrigo Tellez Girón, Master of the Order of Calatrava, who had been hit by two crossbow bolts.

Fortified wall of the hilltop city of Ronda which formed the western bastion of the Amirate of Granada. (Author's photograph)

A general gloom now descended and at a council of war on Saturday evening Fernando decided that their position was untenable and ordered a withdrawal across the Rio Frio to await reinforcements. The first to get this message were the men on the Heights of Albohacen, but as they left the hilltops at dawn on 7 July, their abandoned fortifications were immediately taken by Moorish troops. At this point the rest of the Christian army, seeing Moorish banners on the hill and not apparently having been told about the withdrawal, thought that the enemy were attacking. Panic spread rapidly and there was a disorganised flight towards the Rio Frio.

An experienced campaigner like 'Ali al-'Attâr would not miss such an opportunity and he immediately led the Loja garrison in a general assault on the confused enemy. Fernando now put himself at the head of his guards and, with some other cavalry, occupied raised ground from which to resist the Moorish sortie. A squadron of Castilian men-at-arms under the Marquis of Cadiz also charged the Moorish flank, forcing several into the gorge of the Genil. From then on the Moors harried stragglers as they retreated to the Peña de los Enamorados, about 35km away. Meanwhile, the Amir Abû'l-Hassan arrived from Granada and joined in scouring the area. For King Fernando this defeat was a salutary lesson, showing what a determined foe he faced, as well as revealing the inexperience of many Spanish commanders.

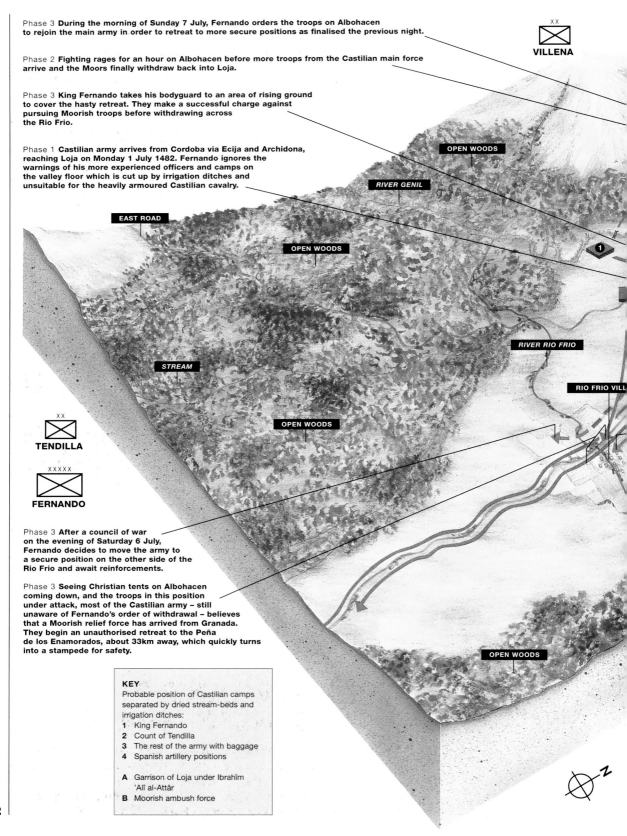

Phase 3 During the morning of Sunday 7 July, Fernando orders the troops on Albohacen to rejoin the main army in order to retreat to more secure positions as finalised the previous night.

Phase 2 Fighting rages for an hour on Albohacen before more troops from the Castilian main force arrive and the Moors finally withdraw back into Loja.

Phase 3 King Fernando takes his bodyguard to an area of rising ground to cover the hasty retreat. They make a successful charge against pursuing Moorish troops before withdrawing across the Rio Frio.

Phase 1 Castilian army arrives from Cordoba via Ecija and Archidona, reaching Loja on Monday 1 July 1482. Fernando ignores the warnings of his more experienced officers and camps on the valley floor which is cut up by irrigation ditches and unsuitable for the heavily armoured Castilian cavalry.

Phase 3 After a council of war on the evening of Saturday 6 July, Fernando decides to move the army to a secure position on the other side of the Rio Frio and await reinforcements.

Phase 3 Seeing Christian tents on Albohacen coming down, and the troops in this position under attack, most of the Castilian army – still unaware of Fernando's order of withdrawal – believes that a Moorish relief force has arrived from Granada. They begin an unauthorised retreat to the Peña de los Enamorados, about 33km away, which quickly turns into a stampede for safety.

VILLENA

OPEN WOODS

RIVER GENIL

EAST ROAD

OPEN WOODS

RIVER RIO FRIO

RIO FRIO VILL

STREAM

OPEN WOODS

TENDILLA

FERNANDO

OPEN WOODS

KEY
Probable position of Castilian camps separated by dried stream-beds and irrigation ditches:
1 King Fernando
2 Count of Tendilla
3 The rest of the army with baggage
4 Spanish artillery positions

A Garrison of Loja under Ibrahîm 'Alî al-Attâr
B Moorish ambush force

42

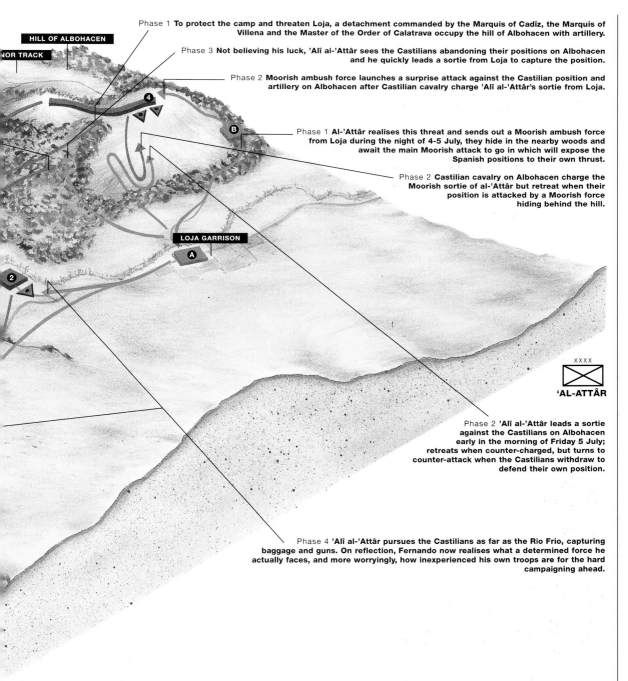

HILL OF ALBOHACEN

NOR TRACK

LOJA GARRISON

Phase 1 **To protect the camp and threaten Loja, a detachment commanded by the Marquis of Cadiz, the Marquis of Villena and the Master of the Order of Calatrava occupy the hill of Albohacen with artillery.**

Phase 3 **Not believing his luck, 'Alî al-'Attâr sees the Castilians abandoning their positions on Albohacen and he quickly leads a sortie from Loja to capture the position.**

Phase 2 **Moorish ambush force launches a surprise attack against the Castilian position and artillery on Albohacen after Castilian cavalry charge 'Alî al-'Attâr's sortie from Loja.**

Phase 1 **Al-'Attâr realises this threat and sends out a Moorish ambush force from Loja during the night of 4-5 July, they hide in the nearby woods and await the main Moorish attack to go in which will expose the Spanish positions to their own thrust.**

Phase 2 **Castilian cavalry on Albohacen charge the Moorish sortie of al-'Attâr but retreat when their position is attacked by a Moorish force hiding behind the hill.**

XXXX

'AL-ATTÂR

Phase 2 **'Alî al-'Attâr leads a sortie against the Castilians on Albohacen early in the morning of Friday 5 July; retreats when counter-charged, but turns to counter-attack when the Castilians withdraw to defend their own position.**

Phase 4 **'Alî al-'Attâr pursues the Castilians as far as the Rio Frio, capturing baggage and guns. On reflection, Fernando now realises what a determined force he actually faces, and more worryingly, how inexperienced his own troops are for the hard campaigning ahead.**

THE DEFEAT OF FERNANDO OUTSIDE LOJA (1-7 JULY 1482)

Viewed from the south-west. Castile's first major expedition of the war against Loja was more to bolster her prestige. However, with the majority of his troops inexperienced at fighting the Moors and his camps dangerously exposed over a wide area, Fernando left himself open to attack. The Moors seized the intiative, driving the Castilians off their hilltop positions and forcing Fernando to hastily withdraw the following day. This move quickly turned into a rout as the Spaniards sped back towards the Rio Frio.

When Abû'l-Hassan arrived at Loja, he heard that his son Muhammad had rebelled and seized power in Granada. Muhammad XII, or 'Boabdil' as he is widely known, seems to have represented a peace faction which preferred an accommodation with Fernando and Isabel rather than tackling Spanish aggression head-on. As a result the Amirate was divided between the supporters of Muhammad XII in Granada and those of Abû'l-Hassan in Malaga. There were no further large-scale operations during the rest of 1482, though both sides conducted cross-border raids. At the same time Spanish preparations for the war against the Moors continued with efforts to reform the *Hermandad*. The Papacy also sent money to support what was coming to be seen as a Crusade.

The next active step was another major defeat — this time of Castile's experienced Andalusian commanders. On the advice of his scouts Don Alfonso de Cárdenas, Grand Master of Santiago who commanded the Ecija frontier zone, planned to march directly across the sparsely popu-

Pinos Puenta, the medieval bridge over the Rio Cubillas which was the scene of many bitter combats during the final war for Granada. (Author's photograph)

lated Ajarquía Sierras, ravage the area around the Amirate's main port of Malaga and then return westward along the coast. He had also been told that there were very few enemy cavalry in the Malaga garrison.

This plan was supported by several frontier lords and experts, including the Marquis of Cadiz. They assembled their men at Antequera where they were joined by militias from the Andalusian cities. Meanwhile, the Marquis of Cadiz received more accurate information via his own intelligence system and advised limiting the target to the mountain village of Almogia, but he was overruled by the proud Grand Master of Santiago and other young knights eager for glory. So, on Wednesday 19 March 1483, the army set out, presumably taking the steep track past the peak of Camorro then down the narrow valley of the Rio Campanillas. Its vanguard was led by the *Adelantado* or Captain General Enrique and Don Alfonso de Aguilar, the centre being under the Marquis of Cadiz and the Count of Cifuentes, while the Grand Master of Santiago commanded the rearguard. Most of the troops were cavalry, including the best in Andalusia, with only a few foot soldiers. Though they had no

The high sierras inland from Malaga are some of the wildest country in southern Spain. In these valleys a large Castilian raiding force was destroyed by the Muslim garrison of Malaga. (Author's photograph)

The massive Alcazaba of Malaga overlooks the city while itself being overlooked by a citadel on the Gibralfaro hill. (Author's photograph)

artillery and little baggage, they were encumbered by a large number of camp followers hoping for rich pickings. They travelled by night, so progress was slow.

The invaders plundered and burned what little they found in the mountains, the smoke of their passage soon being visible to the Malaga garrison which, despite Spanish intelligence, included a large number of cavalry under the Amir Abû'l-Hassan. Impetuous as usual, the old Amir wanted to attack the invaders immediately, but his more cautious younger brother Muhammad (later Amir Muhammad XIII al-Zagal) dissuaded him. Instead al-Zagal took a small force of picked horsemen to engage the Castilians in the valleys behind Malaga, while a larger force commanded by Abû'l-Hassan turned the enemy's flank by seizing the heights around them. This force also included the best crossbowmen and handgunners under Ridwân 'Benegas' (possibly Ibn Ayas) who was of Christian origin and featured in Moorish ballads as an ideal knight in love and war.

The Castilians' discipline was deteriorating and only the Grand Master of Santiago seemed able to keep his men in a proper order. Other small parties scattered to plunder, some young knights approaching the walls of Malaga itself to demonstrate their contempt for the Moors. At this point, al-Zagal suddenly emerged from a side valley to attack the Castilian rear. The Knights of Santiago retained their cohesion, but the broken terrain was more suited to Moorish tactics, and even the rearguard began to fall apart. The Grand Master sent an urgent message to the Marquis of Cadiz, requesting help. The marquis gathered as

many of his men as possible before riding back up the valley in support. An experienced campaigner against the Moors, the marquis wanted to lure the enemy into an open part of the valley suited to the Castilians' armoured horsemen, but the equally adept al-Zagal withdrew his own men into the mountains.

During this crisis the centre and vanguard reassembled and the Castilian commanders held a council of war. Their position was dangerous: they were facing a stronger enemy than expected, hemmed into a valley and with the entire countryside up in arms. But should they return the way they had come or should they risk marching past the garrisoned city of Malaga to take the easier coastal road? Their guides urged the former and so the Castilians retraced their steps. It was now late afternoon, they were burdened with plunder and the Muslims harassed them continuously as the valley grew narrower, the thickets denser, the slopes steeper. Finally the raiding force realised that it was lost in a deep ravine where even the infantry found the going difficult.

Their only hope of escape lay in finding their original route, so the Castilians abandoned their loot and again retraced their steps. As night

DEFEAT OF THE SPANISH IN THE MOUNTAINS OF MALAGA

It was night when the Moorish garrison of Malaga closed in on the Spanish raiders. By the light of firebrands they poured arrows, crossbow bolts, javelins, gunfire and rocks down on the confused enemy who soon panicked, leaving huge numbers dead or captured. One of those who seems to have abandoned his followers was the Master of the Order of Santiago. Like most of those lucky enough to escape he made his way across mountains and deep ravines before reaching friendly territory.

fell the Moors lit bonfires to guide their own reinforcements and to illuminate their enemies. Eventually the thirsty Spaniards reached a small
stream but this was held by enemy troops who rolled rocks onto the
raiders. With no commander able to impose control, the Spaniards dis-
solved into a terrified mob. Seemingly paralysed, it was not until mid-
night that a concerted attempt was made to break out of the valley. As
the Grand Master of Santiago reportedly said to his men, *'Better to lose our
lives in cutting a way through the foe, than be butchered without resistance like
cattle in the slaughterhouse.'*

It was to no avail and, before making his own escape over the crest of
the mountain the proud Grand Master supposedly cried out, *'O God,
great is Your anger this day against Your servants! You have changed the cow-
ardice of these infidels into desperate valour, and have made peasants and oafs
into men of valour.'* The Moors brought back prisoners in droves, and
even the sacred banner of the Order of Santiago was lost that night. The
Count of Cifuentes' division suffered most, and he found himself alone,
surrounded by six Muslim cavalrymen who attacked him until Ridwân
Benegas appeared. He considered the uneven conflict to be an unfair

fight, and told his men to back off while he took on the count alone. The duel did not last long, and the Count of Cifuentes was soon captured. Other Castilians got so lost that they found themselves back near Malaga where they surrendered to women who came out of the city to collect prisoners. Others made their way to the Spanish-held castle of Alhama de Granada after wandering the hills for almost a week, living on wild berries and hiding during the daylight, although the Marquis of Cadiz made his way to Antequera relatively easily.

In Granada Muhammad XII feared that his father's victory might undermine his own support, particularly as King Fernando's forces were now raiding territory under his authority. So Muhammad XII decided to win a victory of his own. He and his most experienced frontier warrior, 'Alî al-'Attâr, left Granada in the middle of April 1483, although Castilian

The defeat of Boabdil's raid against Lucena on one of the carved choir stalls in Toledo Cathedral. Muhammad XII is believed to be the Moor with raised hands and thickly quilted tunic. His best general, the aged 'Alî al-Attâr, is probably lying just to the left. (*in situ*, Cathedral Choir, Toledo)

intelligence sources may already have known that Lucena was to be their target. Unlike the Castilian raiding force which came to grief near Malaga, Muhammad XII's raiders consisted of up to 9,000 infantry and only 700 cavalry as they did intend to besiege Lucena. As they crossed the Castilian frontier, the news was sent by the Alcaide de los Donceles who was in command at Lucena to his uncle, Diego Fernandez de Cordoba, the Count of Cabra. Meanwhile, Moorish cavalry raided as far as Aguilar on the road to Cordoba before joining the siege of Lucena.

The Count of Cabra led a small force of infantry and cavalry to help his nephew. Muslim scouts overestimated its size, so Muhammad XII raised the siege on 20 April and withdrew towards the frontier, but the Moors' progress was now slowed by booty and prisoners. When the Spaniards made contact, the Muslims reassembled quickly, while their

cavalry formed into two units. They then moved toward the Rio Genil, Muhammad XII being prominent on a white horse surrounded by his bodyguard. The Spaniards attacked and, although the Moors saw them coming, the enemy numbers were obscured by morning mist. Consequently, the Muslims thought they were being attacked by a much larger army and decided to make a fighting retreat.

At this point the Spanish infantry who were stationed in a wooded grove while their cavalry charged from the opposite side of the valley, shouted, *'Remember the Mountains of Malaga!'* This strengthened the impression of a larger force so that the Moors continued to fall back while their cavalry kept the Christians at bay. The only practical ford seems to have been near the village of Fuentes de Cesna, a name which came from the Arabic *Ayn al-Hisn* or 'spring of the castle'. In April, even small rivers could rise suddenly as a result of rain far away, and suddenly Muhammad XII's raiding army found its retreat obstructed by the swollen ford. The cavalry covered the infantry as the latter struggled across the rising river, with the Amir Muhammad XII's own guard stationed in trees near the riverbank. Things remained under control until the aged 'Alî al-'Attâr was struck down, and the Moors' famous discipline failed. Those who got across the river raced for the safety of Loja and seeing this, the Castilians attacked more fiercely, targeting the Amir's cavalry guard who now found it impossible to cross the swollen river. Instead, they dismounted to make a final stand, 50 being killed while

Muhammad XII was wounded and tried to hide in reed beds next to the river. There he was confronted by an ordinary Spanish soldier named Martin Hurtado before two more Spanish infantrymen appeared. Muhammad XII offered them a large amount of money if they let him escape, whereupon Don Diego Fernandez de Cordoba rode up. The foot soldiers said, 'Señor, here is a Moor we have taken, who seems to be a man of rank and offers a large ransom,' but the wounded Amir shouted, *'Serfs! You have not taken me. I surrender only to this knight.'* As a result of this success the Counts of Cabra were permitted to add a crowned Moor's head with gold chain around his neck to their coat-of-arms.

RAIDING AND COUNTER-RAIDING

The events of 1482–3 were followed by two years of manoeuvring. By capturing Muhammad XII, Fernando and Isabel were able to meddle directly in Granada's complex political situation. King Fernando hurried south and Muhammad XII was taken to Cordoba and treated with great courtesy. Flattered by such attention, the young ruler agreed a peace treaty, and Fernando and Isabel freed him on 2 September. Peace was still a fragile gamble, however, for Muhammad XII and his father Abû'l-Hassan might still have forgotten their differences and joined forces to defend the Amirate against the Spanish. It may also have been at this point that Fernando and Isabel realised that the total conquest of Granada was a real possibility.

Civil war between the rival Amirs seemed to be doing the Spaniards' work for them. Nevertheless, the Moors fought back early in September 1483 when Abû'l-Hassan launched a raid intended to increase his prestige in comparison to that of his son. The garrisons of Malaga and Ronda combined to carry out an ambitious raid towards Utrera, three-quarters of the way towards the Castilians' chief southern city of Cordoba. Its 1,500 cavalry and 4,000 infantry were led by Bashîr, the grey-haired commander of the Malaga garrison, and troops from Ronda commanded by Hamîd al-Zagrî.

This expedition involved elaborate strategy with most of Bashîr's infantry left in the mountain pass near the Rio Guadalete supported by a cavalry ambush at the Rio Lopera, while the rest of the cavalry spread across Castilian territory doing as much damage as possible. Having supposedly been warned by Christian bandits in the mountains, the garrisons of Ecija, Utrera and other towns assembled near Jerez. They then pursued the raiders, who consisted largely of North African volunteers led by Hamîd al-Zagrî, only to be attacked by Bashîr's cavalry ambush and by the raiders on 17 September. But Bashîr was captured and the two Moorish groups divided. The Spaniards, however, did not split their forces and instead defeated the smaller Moorish band of cavalry near Lopera.

THE DEATH OF 'ALÎ AL-'ATTÂR
Muhammad XII, 'Boabdil', led a raid towards Lucena to compete with al-Zagal's recent triumph near Malaga. Not only was his force defeated while trying to cross a swollen river near Fuentes de Cesna, but Muhammad XII was captured and his loyal ally, 'Alî al-'Attâr, was killed. This highly experienced old warrior in his eighties is said to have gone down fighting.

A large Spanish force under the Marquis of Cadiz now attacked the Moors as they attempted to rally near the Guadalete, defeating them and then overrunning the infantry who were defending the mountain pass. Meanwhile, the first Moorish cavalry force under Hamîd al-Zagrî broke off contact and reassembled on the wrong side of the Rio Guadalete. Their path home was blocked, so they made a wide sweep through enemy territory, riding by night and hiding by day, across the Guadalete, past Arcos and back into the Sierra de Ronda close by the scene of the previous Moorish defeat. To follow up this somewhat unexpected success, the Castilians retook Zahara late in October. That month the legal authorities in Granada issued a *fatwa* or judgement denying Muhammad XII the right to rule as Amir because he was now widely seen as a tool of the infidels. Some months later, the Spanish government warned Genoa and Venice that their merchants would suffer if Italian ships ferried Muslim reinforcements from North Africa to Granada.

In the spring of 1484 the Spaniards launched a large and much more successful raid, devastating the area around Alora, Coin, Cazaraboncla, Almexia and Cartama in a ten-day operation. The raiders then moved on to the fertile Vega of Malaga where they were resupplied by Spanish ships lying off-shore. The next 40 days saw the same raiders carve a swathe of destruction back to Antequera. In June Fernando himself took command of this army, increasing its size and adding artillery before marching against Alora which fell on 20 June. Yet when refugees arrived in Malaga from Alora, their accounts of the power of Spanish artillery were not believed. Now Fernando led a third raid, leaving some troops to sup-

RIGHT **Aragonese soldiers and a *mudejar* horseman emerging from the city of Palma de Mallorca, as shown on the *Retable of St George* by Pere Nissart, 1468-80. (PMM 122, Museu Diocesà de Mallorca, Palma)**

BELOW **The little town of Medina Sidonia seen from its ruined castle. It was the target of several Moorish raids. (Author's photograph)**

port Muhammad XII in the city of Granada, though it seems that the port of Almeria was now Muhammad XII's main centre of power, and on 20 September Fernando took the strong frontier fortress of Setenil.

A TURBAN OF CLOUDS

In January 1485 an *Auto da Fé* was held in Seville where 19 men and women were burned at the stake, bringing the total of those killed by the Inquisition in this area for various forms of 'heresy' to 500. It was a grim omen for the future of those who, like the Muslims of Granada, continued to defy the might of King Fernando, Queen Isabel and the Catholic Church.

The Amirate of Granada began to suffer major losses of territory in 1485. King Fernando now had sufficient large artillery to take cities, but the substantial army which took the field on 5 April first crushed a muslim rebellion at Benamaquex. Having taken the town by storm,

the Muslim Amirate of Granada,
the power of Spanish artillery
was more obvious than divine
aid. Even so, the Spaniards had
little technological advantage
over their enemies. What they
did have were larger economic
resources and rulers determined
to crush the last Muslim state in
the Iberia.

Fernando hung 101 of its leading citizens from the walls, while the rest
of the population were enslaved. Next, he secured his communications
down the Guadalhorce Valley, stationing himself between Coin and
Cartama, while the Marquis of Cadiz attacked the first and Don Alfonso
de Aguilar the second. In response Muhammad XIII al-Zagal assembled
his troops in the mountain village of Monda in an attempt to relieve
these towns, while Hamîd al-Zagrî arrived with the garrison of Ronda
and after bitter fighting broke into Coin. Both places fell: Coin on 27
April and Cartama on the 28th, Hamîd al-Zagrî and his North African
volunteers being permitted to leave with their weapons.

Early in May, Fernando made a brief raid towards Malaga where al-
Zagal had prepared strong defences, resulting in savage fighting in the
orchards around the city. Fernando was now informed by Yûsuf
Sharîfah, a leading citizen of Ronda, that the city was weakly defended
so he changed his objective and led his army on a secret march to that
western bastion of the Amirate of Granada. Ronda was built in an aston-
ishingly strong defensive position and, as an earlier Arab visitor had put

it, had *'clouds for a turban and a torrential river for a sword-belt'*. It was normally garrisoned by North African volunteers commanded by Hamîd al-Zagrî, but, knowing that Fernando planned to attack Malaga, Hamîd had organised a raid into Castilian territory around Medina Sidonia. He took personal command while also sending another part of the garrison to help defend Malaga. It was a successful raid, but as Hamîd al-Zagrî and his troops returned they heard artillery and saw that their own city was now besieged by Fernando.

Despite several determined attempts they could not break through the Spanish siege-lines and during this stalemate the Marquis of Cadiz began negotiations with leading civilians inside Ronda led by one of the chief bailiffs, probably Ibrâhîm al-Hakîm. On 18 May the Spaniards cut the famous rock stairway from the river up to the city, severing Ronda's supply of drinking water, while the Spanish bombardment started several fires in the city. On 22 May Ronda surrendered, Ibrâhîm al-Hakîm and other members of the civilian élite being allowed to settle near Seville as Hamîd al-Zagrî with the rest of his troops went to join the garrison of Malaga.

CONFUSION IN GRANADA

The fall of Ronda was followed by the collapse of most of the western part of the Amirate, including the naval base at Marbella. This expansion of Spanish naval facilities probably contributed to the Sultan of Morocco's willingness to sign a treaty of friendship with Spain in 1485. In addition, Venetian and Genoese merchant ships were ordered not to sell English copper and tin to the Moors when returning from their annual trading voyage to Britain.

The disasters of 1485 contributed to the stroke suffered by Abû'l-Hassan 'Alî, his role as one of the two rival Amirs being taken over by his younger brother al-Zagal, who became known as Muhammad XIII. Muhammad al-Zagal had already led a daring attempt to capture his nephew in Almeria in February. He failed, though Muhammad XII again fled to the safety of Castilian territory. From then on Muhammad XII 'Boabdil' also became widely known as al-Zuguybî, 'the Unlucky'.

Muhammad XIII al-Zagal marched from Malaga to Granada to make good his claim to be Amir and on the way he virtually wiped out a foraging party of Knights of the Order of Calatrava from Castilian-held Alhama. From then on Muslim resistance stiffened under his capable leadership. At the end of August three separate groups of Spanish troops marched to attack Moclin, guarding the northern passes to Granada. But the first, under the Count of Cabra, was diverted by what looked like a chance to capture al-Zagal – the count having previously captured Muhammad XII 'Boabdil'. The Spanish were ambushed and the Count of Cabra was wounded by a handgun, though his troops were saved from utter rout by the arrival of the second Spanish force under the Master of Calatrava and the Bishop of Jaen. While Muhammad XIII al-Zagal entered Moclin in triumph, the Spanish retreated to Fuente de los Reyes to join the third force under King Fernando. Uncertain what to do, Fernando suddenly got a letter from his wife advising him to forget Moclin and instead to attack the castles of Cambil and Albahar held by the powerful Moorish Banû al-Sarrâj family, and which had long threatened the town of Jaen.

The Sierra Nevada mountains overlooking the Vega of Granada, photographed in late spring. (Author's photograph)

Here the Moorish defenders believed that it was impossible to bring heavy siege artillery against such naturally impregnable positions. Two thousand cavalry under the Marquis of Cadiz first came over the mountains to invest the castles. Queen Isabel moved her headquarters to Jaen while Fernando arrived more slowly with the rest of the army. The castles were commanded by Muhammad Ibn Yûsuf al-Sarrâj who was confident of his ability to resist any normal assault. Then, however, he is said to have heard strange sounds in the hills; it was Spanish pioneers cutting a road for their heavy artillery. Once the guns arrived the bombardment began and some of the biggest artillery was hauled onto a hill overlooking both castles. But before they opened fire, Muhammad Ibn Yûsuf al-Sarrâj recognised the inevitable, and surrendered Cambil and Albahar on 23 September 1485. A few days earlier the Spanish garrison at Alhama de Granada unexpectedly took the castle of Zalea with the help of a traitor within its walls.

Around this time Fernando and Isabel allowed Muhammad XII 'Boabdil' to return to Granada yet again, though the young Amir's usefulness as an ally was limited because he had so little support. At first he seemed to turn against his Spanish friends by making peace with his uncle, the rival Amir Muhammad XIII al-Zagal, and offering to defend Loja on his behalf. Quite why al-Zagal agreed is unknown, for when Fernando led his troops against Loja Muhammad XII was defeated. He may even have been playing the traitor, though he was reportedly wounded during the siege. Hamîd al-Zagrî was also there, perhaps to keep an eye on the unreliable 'Boabdil', and was more seriously injured. Late in May the town and citadel both surrendered. Hamîd al-Zagrî and the garrison were allowed to leave, while Muhammad XII 'Boabdil' was taken prisoner, perhaps for his own safety.

King Fernando then took his army against Illora which fell in June after a brave defence. The inhabitants were escorted to the bridge at Pinos Puente which had, in effect, become the new front-line 15km from Granada. In strategic terms the city of Granada had lost its outer shield and now stood virtually alone. Fernando was confident enough to ask Queen Isabel to visit the army, she and her ladies being met at Peña de los Enamorados by an escort under the Marquis of Cadiz before joining Fernando with great ceremony outside Illora on 11 June 1486. Her arrival was described in loving detail by the chroniclers, even down to the details of her dress: a scarlet cloak of Moorish design, velvet outerskirts, velvet and brocade underskirts, broad brimmed black hat with thick embroidery, hair in a silk net, and riding a brown mule blanketed with gold-embroidered satin with a richly gilded silver. Fernando apparently rode a fine horse and wore a crimson shirt, a loose brocade robe over short yellow skirts, a plumed hat and a sabre. The campaign seemed to be becoming a triumphal procession with all the elaborate display of late medieval chivalry, but in reality there were more than five years to go.

That summer the *qa'ids* or governors of Moclin and Illora, who were brothers, begged Muhammad XIII al-Zagal for a chance to hit back at the enemy raiding the Vega of Granada. He agreed, and Fernando's advance guard were attacked at Piños Puente. It was another bitter fight which entered Andalusian folklore. The Count of Cabra was nearly captured, but the Moors

BELOW **Another detail from the *Retable of St George* by Pere Nissart, 1468-80, showing the Catalan-Aragonese army landing supplies outside Palma. (PMM 122, Museu Diocesà de Mallorca, Palma)**

EVENTS 1486-1489

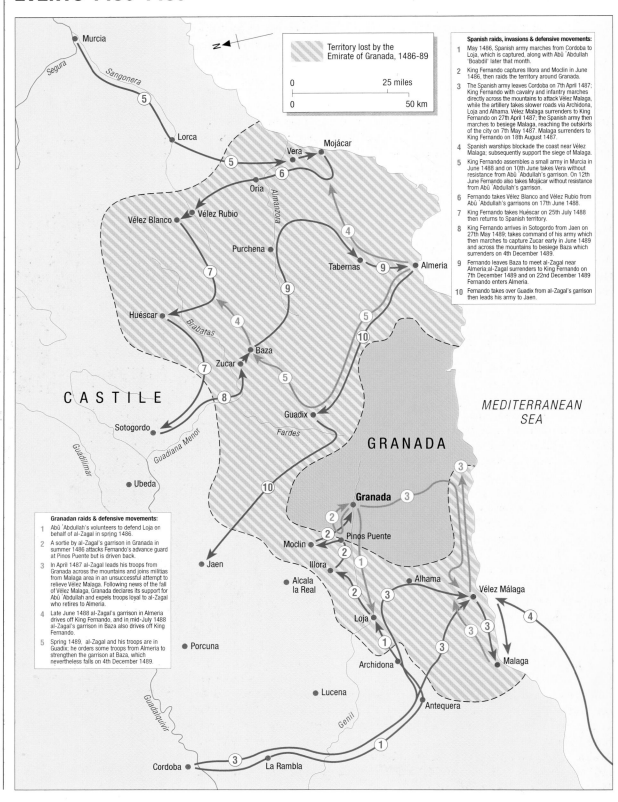

Territory lost by the Emirate of Granada, 1486-89

0		25 miles
0		50 km

Spanish raids, invasions & defensive movements:

1 May 1486, Spanish army marches from Cordoba to Loja, which is captured, along with Abû ʿAbdullah 'Boabdil' later that month.

2 King Fernando captures Illora and Moclin in June 1486, then raids the territory around Granada.

3 The Spanish army leaves Cordoba on 7th April 1487; King Fernando with cavalry and infantry marches directly across the mountains to attack Vélez Malaga, while the artillery takes slower roads via Archidona, Loja and Alhama. Vélez Malaga surrenders to King Fernando on 27th April 1487; the Spanish army then marches to besiege Malaga, reaching the outskirts of the city on 7th May 1487. Malaga surrenders to King Fernando on 18th August 1487.

4 Spanish warships blockade the coast near Vélez Malaga; subsequently support the siege of Malaga.

5 King Fernando assembles a small army in Murcia in June 1488 and on 10th June takes Vera without resistance from Abû ʿAbdullah's garrison. On 12th June Fernando also takes Mojácar without resistance from Abû ʿAbdullah's garrison.

6 Fernando takes Vélez Blanco and Vélez Rubio from Abû ʿAbdullah's garrisons on 17th June 1488.

7 King Fernando takes Huéscar on 25th July 1488 then returns to Spanish territory.

8 King Fernando arrives in Sotogordo from Jaen on 27th May 1489; takes command of his army which then marches to capture Zucar early in June 1489 and across the mountains to besiege Baza which surrenders on 4th December 1489.

9 Fernando leaves Baza to meet al-Zagal near Almeria;al-Zagal surrenders to King Fernando on 7th December 1489 and on 22nd December 1489 Fernando enters Almeria.

10 Fernando takes over Guadix from al-Zagal's garrison then leads his army to Jaen.

Granadan raids & defensive movements:

1 Abû ʿAbdullah's volunteers to defend Loja on behalf of al-Zagal in spring 1486.

2 A sortie by al-Zagal's garrison in Granada in summer 1486 attacks Fernando's advance guard at Pinos Puente but is driven back.

3 In April 1487 al-Zagal leads his troops from Granada across the mountains and joins militias from Malaga area in an unsuccessful attempt to relieve Vélez Malaga. Following news of the fall of Vélez Malaga, Granada declares its support for Abû ʿAbdullah and expels troops loyal to al-Zagal who retires to Almeria.

4 Late June 1488 al-Zagal's garrison in Almeria drives off King Fernando, and in mid-July 1488 al-Zagal's garrison in Baza also drives off King Fernando.

5 Spring 1489, al-Zagal and his troops are in Guadix; he orders some troops from Almeria to strengthen the garrison at Baza, which nevertheless falls on 4th December 1489.

were finally driven back, the brother *qa'ids* dying in defence of the bridge, while their men escaped. Elsewhere the Moors opened the sluice-gates of their irrigation system, flooding the area and almost trapping the Bishop of Jaen. The Spaniards, however, did enormous damage before returning to Moclin at the end of summer.

Fernando now drew up another agreement with Muhammad XII 'Boabdil'. This time Muhammad agreed to accept the title of Duke of Baza, Guadix and lordship of several other towns in the north-east of the Amirate – providing he himself conquered them. Fernando released 'Boabdil' to further divide Muslim loyalties and this time, Muhammad XII remained a reasonably loyal vassal of the Spanish rulers for three years. On 15 September 1486 he and his remaining followers, supported by Spanish troops, entered the Albaicin quarter on the northern side of Granada, while al-Zagal's garrison were holed up in the fortified Alhambra Palace. Civil war in the streets followed as Muhammad XII and Muhammad XIII fought for control of the city. This constant skirmishing within Granada hindered Muhammad XIII al-Zagal's ability to fight the Spanish invaders for three years, while the conquest of remaining Granadan territory took on a more planned character with the steady reduction of town and fortresses.

14th-15th century brigandine of iron scales covered with an outer layer of red velvet. (Estruch Collection, Barcelona)

THE AMIRATE REDUCED BY HALF

On 7 April 1487 a large Spanish army, largely consisting of Andalusian militias, left Cordoba to march right across Granadan territory towards the strongly fortified town of Vélez Málaga close to the coast. An earthquake the night before they left was interpreted as a sign that Granada would soon fall. The Spaniards' ultimate target was Malaga, but first Vélez Malaga, one of the main coastal defences of Granada, had to be taken to isolate Malaga itself. After passing the old Castilian frontier base at Antequera, the Spaniards separated into two columns. Cavalry and light infantry went over the mountains, while the artillery, with adequate protection and pioneers to clear the way, followed the valleys wherever possible. It was hard going for both forces, with the rivers swollen by rain, and the artillery facing a mountain pass whichever way they went.

Portuguese breastplate of 1460-90, with a cross deeply beaten into the front. (Rainer Daehnhardt Collection, Lisbon)

While the Spanish fleet blockaded the nearby mouth of the Rio de Vélez at what was then called al-Millâha, Fernando's force made camp near Vélez Malaga on Easter Monday 1487, upriver from the town and on a hill positioned to cut the road across the Sierra Tekeda to Granada. This position was, however, *'overlooked by another Muslim castle'*, which may have been at the modern hamlet of Rubite whose name comes from the Arabic *ribât*, though this is not actually in line of sight. Local Moorish militias also gathered on the hills of Bentomiz overlooking both Vélez Malaga and Fernando's camp.

59

A lustre-ware bowl made by 15th century Muslim craftsmen, probably in the city port of Malaga. This type of vessel was equally at home in the Christian or Islamic western Mediterranean. (Victoria and Albert Museum, London)

Conditions in Granada made it extremely difficult for Muhammad XIII al-Zagal to challenge the Spanish attack, and when he did try to raise the siege he had to leave a substantial garrison in the Alhambra to watch Muhammad XII in the city below. Furthermore, 'Boabdil' had supporters near Vélez Malaga who co-operated with the Spaniards. Al-Zagal's only hope was to destroy Fernando's heavy artillery before it could bombard Vélez Malaga. Before that happened, however, Fernando's advance force surrounded the town and citadel with linked outposts. During this operation some infantry, sent to occupy a hill close to the walls, were attacked by Moorish cavalry who had not come from Vélez Malaga. They were probably the garrison of the little *talâ'ia* watch-tower at al-Millâha, recalled to join the troops assembling under Muhammad al-Zagal's command in the hills. King Fernando was at that moment having lunch and had taken off his helmet and sword-belt but, seeing the danger, he grabbed a spear and led his guard to help the foot soldiers. A Moor cut down Fernando's page before the king thrust his spear in the enemy's side. Unable to retrieve this weapon, Fernando reached for his sword only to find that it was not there. Weaponless, King Fernando was protected by his guards until the Moors drew off. Thereafter it was agreed that kings should not expose themselves to danger in this manner, while Fernando promised never again to enter a battle without his sword.

On 25 April the slow-moving Spanish artillery train arrived within half a league of Vélez Malaga. Although it had a strong escort, Fernando sent the Commander of León with a large body of cavalry to give additional protection. It was a good move, for at this point Muhammad XIII al-Zagal launched his attack on the guns from Bentomiz. This was led by Ridwân Benegas who was now *qa'id* or governor of Granada. But when al-Zagal saw Spanish reinforcements approaching, he called off the attack and the artillery reached the siege-lines safely.

Instead, Muhammad XIII al-Zagal decided on a co-ordinated night attack by troops in the hills and the garrison of Vélez Malaga. Perhaps he was hoping that the Spanish guard would be down as they placed their guns in position. Unfortunately his messenger to the garrison, a renegado who might pass himself off as a Christian if intercepted, was captured, recognised and forced to confess al-Zagal's plans. Consequently, the beacon on Bentomiz was not answered by a beacon in Vélez Malaga, but Muhammad XIII al-Zagal decided to attack anyway. As his men advanced, they found the entire Spanish army waiting for them in silence and without any lights. The Moors immediately lit bonfires to illuminate the scene and the rest of the night was taken up with savage fighting.

At dawn the Spaniards made a cautious counter-attack only to find that their foes had been seized by an inexplicable panic, and had scattered towards Granada and Malaga, though Ridwân Benegas led some fugitives into Vélez Malaga. The Spanish bombardment began on 27 April when news also arrived that Muhammad XIII al-Zagal's garrison in the Alhambra of Granada had transferred its allegiance to Muhammad XII

Portuguese sword of the second half of the 15th century. (Alfredo Keil Collection)

Typical late 15th century Spanish sword, again with protection around the *pas d'âne*. (Instituto del Conde Valencia de Don Juan, Madrid)

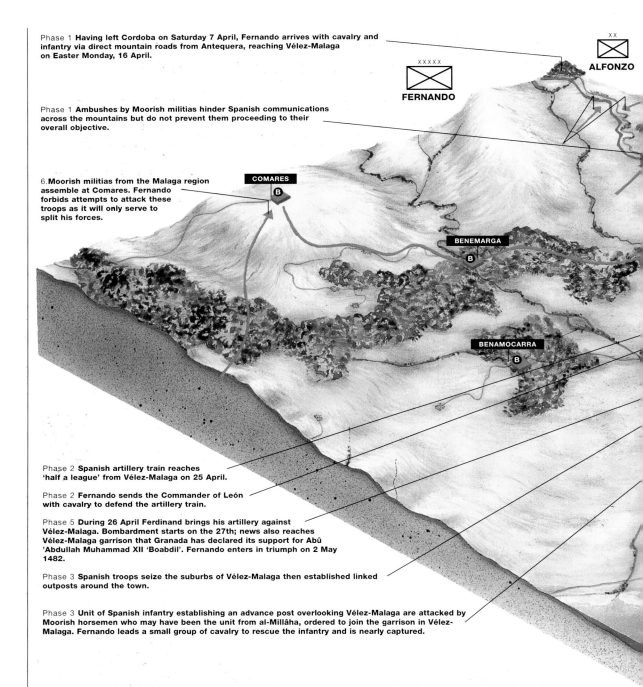

Phase 1 **Having left Cordoba on Saturday 7 April, Fernando arrives with cavalry and infantry via direct mountain roads from Antequera, reaching Vélez-Malaga on Easter Monday, 16 April.**

Phase 1 **Ambushes by Moorish militias hinder Spanish communications across the mountains but do not prevent them proceeding to their overall objective.**

6. **Moorish militias from the Malaga region assemble at Comares. Fernando forbids attempts to attack these troops as it will only serve to split his forces.**

XXXXX
FERNANDO

XX
ALFONZO

COMARES
B

BENEMARGA
B

BENAMOCARRA
B

Phase 2 **Spanish artillery train reaches 'half a league' from Vélez-Malaga on 25 April.**

Phase 2 **Fernando sends the Commander of León with cavalry to defend the artillery train.**

Phase 5 **During 26 April Ferdinand brings his artillery against Vélez-Malaga. Bombardment starts on the 27th; news also reaches Vélez-Malaga garrison that Granada has declared its support for Abû 'Abdullah Muhammad XII 'Boabdil'. Fernando enters in triumph on 2 May 1482.**

Phase 3 **Spanish troops seize the suburbs of Vélez-Malaga then established linked outposts around the town.**

Phase 3 **Unit of Spanish infantry establishing an advance post overlooking Vélez-Malaga are attacked by Moorish horsemen who may have been the unit from al-Millâha, ordered to join the garrison in Vélez-Malaga. Fernando leads a small group of cavalry to rescue the infantry and is nearly captured.**

THE CONQUEST OF VÉLEZ-MÁLAGA (16 APRIL - 2 MAY 1487)

Viewed from the south. With the aim of capturing the Amirate's main port of Malaga and securing the coastline for future attacks, Fernando had to first take nearby Vélez Malaga. Blockading the mouth of the river al-Millâha, the Spaniards then began bringing up their huge artillery train to bombard the city. Al-Zagal's forces were weakened by internal feuding and thus limited to surprise attacks on the Spanish, which were ultimately futile.

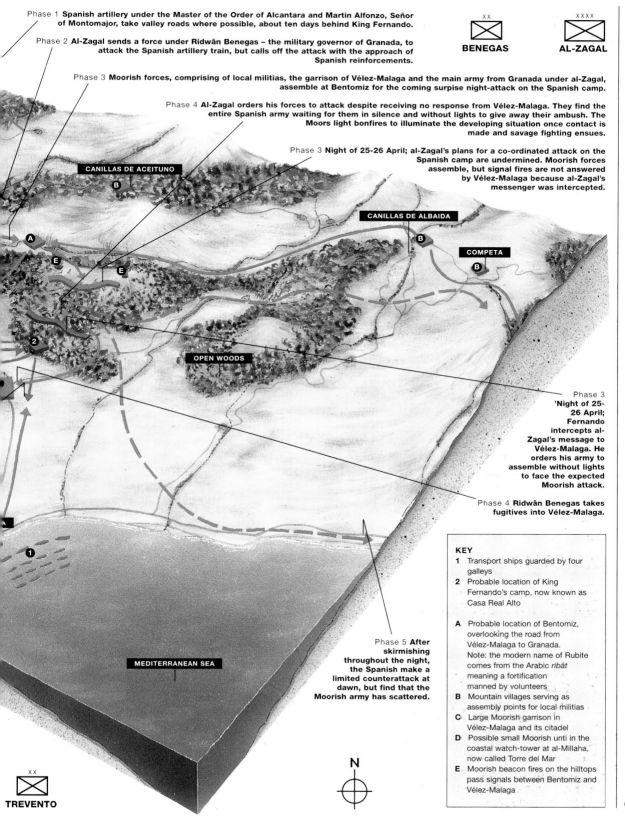

Phase 1 **Spanish artillery under the Master of the Order of Alcantara and Martin Alfonzo, Señor of Montomajor, take valley roads where possible, about ten days behind King Fernando.**

Phase 2 **Al-Zagal sends a force under Ridwân Benegas – the military governor of Granada, to attack the Spanish artillery train, but calls off the attack with the approach of Spanish reinforcements.**

Phase 3 **Moorish forces, comprising of local militias, the garrison of Vélez-Malaga and the main army from Granada under al-Zagal, assemble at Bentomiz for the coming surpise night-attack on the Spanish camp.**

Phase 4 **Al-Zagal orders his forces to attack despite receiving no response from Vélez-Malaga. They find the entire Spanish army waiting for them in silence and without lights to give away their ambush. The Moors light bonfires to illuminate the developing situation once contact is made and savage fighting ensues.**

Phase 3 **Night of 25-26 April; al-Zagal's plans for a co-ordinated attack on the Spanish camp are undermined. Moorish forces assemble, but signal fires are not answered by Vélez-Malaga because al-Zagal's messenger was intercepted.**

Phase 3 **'Night of 25-26 April; Fernando intercepts al-Zagal's message to Vélez-Malaga. He orders his army to assemble without lights to face the expected Moorish attack.**

Phase 4 **Ridwân Benegas takes fugitives into Vélez-Malaga.**

Phase 5 **After skirmishing throughout the night, the Spanish make a limited counterattack at dawn, but find that the Moorish army has scattered.**

BENEGAS

AL-ZAGAL

CANILLAS DE ACEITUNO

CANILLAS DE ALBAIDA

COMPETA

OPEN WOODS

MEDITERRANEAN SEA

TREVENTO

KEY
1 Transport ships guarded by four galleys
2 Probable location of King Fernando's camp, now known as Casa Real Alto

A Probable location of Bentomiz, overlooking the road from Vélez-Malaga to Granada. Note: the modern name of Rubite comes from the Arabic *ribât* meaning a fortification manned by volunteers
B Mountain villages serving as assembly points for local militias
C Large Moorish garrison in Vélez-Malaga and its citadel
D Possible small Moorish unti in the coastal watch-tower at al-Millaha, now called Torre del Mar
E Moorish beacon fires on the hilltops pass signals between Bentomiz and Vélez-Malaga

N

63

'Boabdil'. Consequently even the courageous Ridwân now advised surrender, and on 2 May King Fernando entered Vélez Malaga in triumph.

Muhammad XIII al-Zagal now held only Guadix, Almeria, Baza and Malaga, and Fernando was advancing along the coast with his army, reaching the outer fortifications of Malaga on 7 May. From here the Spaniards had a difficult march inland between a coastal fort and another castle on a hill behind Malaga. The city had three fortresses: the Gibralfaro then known as the *Râbita* on a steep hill on the eastern side of the city, the Alcazaba at the base of this hill joined to the Gibralfaro by doubled walls, and a third unidentified fortification which may have been a temporary affair on what are now the Calvario hills or the Egido hill north of the city.

The Gibralfaro and the Alcazaba were held by Hamîd al-Zagrî's fierce North African garrison, while the third may have been garrisoned by the city militia. For a while efforts by Fernando's household troops and specialist mountaineers from Galicia failed to dislodge the defenders from this minor defensive position, though in the end superior Spanish numbers prevailed. Demands that Hamîd al-Zagrî hand over the city were answered with the bald reply, *'I was sent here to defend, not to surrender'*. His Berber soldiers discouraged talk of peace in Malaga while they and the so-called *renegados* bore the brunt of the fighting.

Both sides had cannon, though the Christian guns were bigger and far more numerous. An enemy cannon-ball hit King Fernando's tent, however, and obliged him to move his camp behind the safety of a nearby hill. The Spaniards also brought additional cannon ashore from their fleet. The resulting bombardment used gunpowder in quantities not seen before, while the attackers pushed their earth and timber emplacements up the steep slope of the Gibralfaro. They included a series of mutually supporting siegeworks called *estanças* (from the Italian word *stanza*), which would later be used in the conquest of the Americas.

The siege was in full swing when, in May, Muhammad XII 'Boabdil' sent a letter from Granada to *'My Lady the Queen Doña Isabel'* requesting a third treaty under which he promised to surrender Granada and his other towns when it was possible for him to do so. In return he asked for Baza, Guadix and other smaller villages. Meanwhile his followers prevented Muhammad XIII al-Zagal supporting Malaga from Almeria. Muslim divisions were as important as Spanish artillery during the decisive year of 1487. At the same time the savagery of the fighting increased: the Church sanctioned parading Moorish heads through the Spanish camp, and Hamîd al-Zagrî authorised an assassination attempt against Fernando and Isabel, who had by now arrived in the Spanish camp. A Muslim ascetic allowed himself to be captured during a sortie and asked to see the Spanish rulers. He was taken to a tent used by Doña Beatriz de Bobadilla, the Marchioness of Moya, and a Portuguese nobleman named Don Alvaro, son of the Duke of Braganza. Seeing this magnificently dressed pair, he mistook them for the king and queen, asked for a drink to distract

15th century heavy Castilian mortar from Burgos with an early example of trunnions. (Museo del Ejército, Madrid)

the guards, then drew a dagger hidden in his clothes. The old ascetic wounded the Portuguese and struck the marchioness before being cut down. As a result, Queen Isabel was given a permanent guard of 200 men-at-arms, while the ascetic's body was cut into pieces and catapulted into Malaga. There the fragments were collected, washed, perfumed and sewn together with silk thread before being given a martyr's funeral.

Still the siege went on. According to the *Nubdhat*, an Arabic history written a few years later, the people of Malaga *'had to eat whatever was edible; horses, asses, donkeys, dogs, even the leaves from the trees'.* But eventually Spanish numbers, artillery and control of the sea took its toll. The North African troops in the Alcazaba still refused to sur-

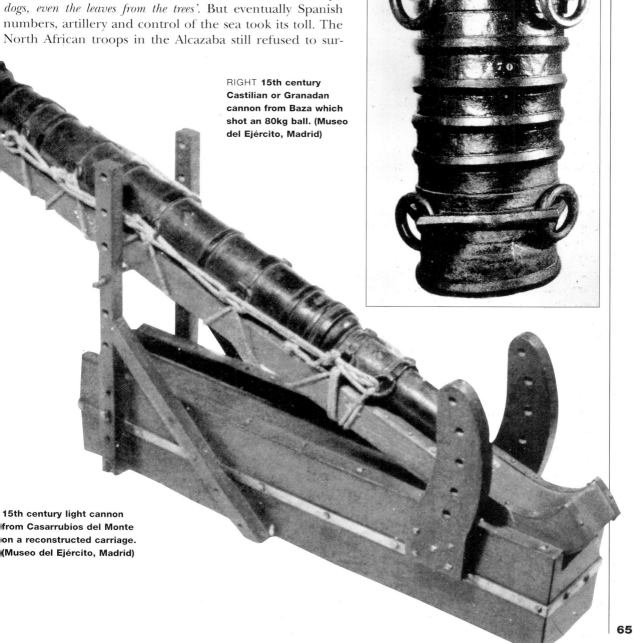

RIGHT **15th century Castilian or Granadan cannon from Baza which shot an 80kg ball. (Museo del Ejército, Madrid)**

15th century light cannon from Casarrubios del Monte on a reconstructed carriage. (Museo del Ejército, Madrid)

65

render, but a party demanding peace emerged from among the civilians led by 'Alî Durdûsh. On 18 August 1487 the city surrendered, followed two days later by Hamîd al-Zagrî's garrison in the fortresses.

The savage treatment meted out to Malaga after this surrender was widely regarded as breaking the established traditions of civilised warfare between Muslims and Christians. Hamîd al-Zagrî was imprisoned in Carmona, along with the city's Jewish population awaiting ransom at 30 gold doblas for each man, woman or child. The great bulk of the Muslim inhabitants of Malaga could not pay, and many were sold as slaves. Around 3,000 surviving soldiers from the garrison were sent to various European rulers as 'gifts' from Fernando and Isabel, 100 men perhaps including Hamîd al-Zagrî being sent to the Pope in Rome. They reportedly arrived during a meeting of the Pope and his cardinals, and were distributed among the assembled clergy as slaves. Others suffered a worse fate. The *renegados,* or Christians who converted to Islam and fought for Granada, were *acañaveados* – in other words used as live targets for cane spears, while captured *conversos* were simply burned at the stake alongside Spanish deserters.

AL-ZAGAL GIVES UP THE STRUGGLE

The capture of Malaga, Granada's second city and main port, completed the conquest of the western half of the Amirate. The end seemed to be in sight and for a while Fernando and Isabel could concentrate on other political problems. Muhammad XII 'Boabdil' was confined to Granada and the relatively infertile regions of Vélez Blanco and Vélez Rubio, but Muhammad XIII al-Zagal still held Baza, Guadix and Almeria which formed the richest part of the state. So for the next two years the Spaniards wore down Muhammad XIII al-Zagal's remaining powerbase.

In June 1488 Fernando assembled a small army in Murcia and crossed into Granadan territory near Muhammad XII 'Boabdil's' town of Vera whose garrison surrendered without a fight. The garrisons of Mojácar, Vélez Blanco and Vélez Rubio did the same. Fernando next marched to Almeria where Muhammad XIII al-Zagal's garrison drove him off. Next the little army went to Baza where they were badly cut up by a Moorish force under al-Zagal himself, before Fernando returned homeward, taking Huescar on 25 July. All this campaign achieved was the capture of a few places belonging to Muhammad XIII who probably expected them to be returned as part of his treaty with Fernando. Instead of fighting, Muhammad XII 'Boabdil' executed five leading religious scholars in Granada for daring to dispute his right to rule. In response, Muhammad XIII al-Zagal raided Castilian territory while using his garrisons at Almeria, Salobreña and in the Purchena Valley to raid around Murcia. Spanish involvement in the intrigue which permeated

Moorish politics was more effective. Lavish bribery even won over al-Zagal's brother-in-law Yahyâ al-Naiyâr, who was later to become one of the leading Moorish collaborators. Yet Muhammad XIII al-Zagal himself continued to resist as fiercely as ever.

The campaign of 1489 was in much the same area but on a far larger scale. On 27 May Fernando took command of a large army at Sotogordo which took Zujar after a desperate resistance, and then marched over the mountains to Baza. Al-Zagal remained at Guadix to guard against any attacks by Muhammad XII 'Boabdil', but ordered Sîdi Yahyâ al-Naiyâr to take some troops from Almeria to strengthen Baza. Here the citadel's natural position made it virtually invulnerable to artillery, while the villas built by Baza's richest citizens around the town had been converted into small fortresses.

The result was bitter fighting for control of the fertile Vega around Baza, with the heroic Ridwân Zalfarga to the fore. This may have been the same man as Ridwân Benegas. The Spanish won, but found that the place they selected for their camp was unsuitable. To abandon it would be dangerous, so they left their tents close to the city while the rest withdrew back to where they started. In this crisis King Fernando again sent a letter to his wife Queen Isabel, asking for advice. This single-minded lady urged him to keep trying, so two new camps were established, one each side of Baza but separated by dense orchards well suited to enemy ambushes. It was a mark of the Spaniards' determination that they sent 4,000 *taladores* or pioneers to cut down all the trees. This took seven weeks, and afterwards the two camps were linked by a moat filled with water diverted from a mountain stream and defended by a palisade with little forts made of earth. Worse still, the Spaniards dug a dry ditch defended by a dry-stone wall right around the other side of the city, isolating it entirely.

While the determined Moorish garrison fought on, the siege was exhausting Spanish finances to such an extent that Queen Isabel had to pawn her jewels. On 7 November Queen Isabel arrived in the besiegers' camp to revive the soldiers' morale and to convince the Moors that their enemies would never go away. Fernando also ordered the construction of a thousand huts and a proper market so that the besiegers could survive the coming winter. Torrential rain swept most of these away, but still the Spaniards would not give up. Muhammad XIII al-Zagal had been unable to relieve Baza, Muhammad XII 'Boabdil' in Granada made no effort to help, and in August the ruler of Fez in Morocco had renewed his treaty with the Portuguese. Now the garrison sent Yahyâ al-Naiyâr to ask al-Zagal's permission to surrender. He reluctantly agreed and on 4 December Baza was handed over.

This time the defenders were treated well, perhaps because they were natives of Granada rather than Africans like the garrison at Malaga. Sîdi Yahyâ al-Naiyâr asked to enter Queen Isabel's service and was sent to al-Zagal in the hope of winning him over. On 7 December Fernando met the Amir and the two men rode together into Almeria. Al-Zagal now recognised the inevitable, signed a treaty with Fernando and Isabel and was in return recognised as the autonomous 'king' of Andaraz in the Alhaurin valley. Some time later al-Zagal's brother-in-law Yahyâ al-Naiyâr converted to Christianity and took the new name of Don Pedro de Granada. As an Arabic chronicle, the *Nubdhat al-'Asr*, put it; '*All this was*

The upper tower of the citadel of Vélez Malaga. It would have been here that the Moorish garrison kept a beacon to communicate with al-Zagal's troops in the hills during King Fernando's siege. (Author's photograph)

with a view to taking revenge on the son of his brother Muhammad Ibn 'Alî and his commanders who had remained in Granada, with just the city under their government and with the benefit of a truce from the enemy. By his action he wanted to cut Granada off, so as to destroy it in the way that the rest of the country had been destroyed.'

It had been a difficult campaign but Muhammad XIII al-Zagal was out of the contest and Muhammad XII 'Boabdil' was expected to surrender, as agreed in his treaty with the Spanish rulers. But he did not. Instead Muhammad XII 'Boabdil' bowed to the wishes of his people who included huge numbers of refugees from areas conquered by the Christians and transformed himself into the hero of Moorish resistance. He may, in fact, have felt that Fernando's seizure of towns owing allegiance to him was a betrayal.

Muhammad XII sent raiding forces across the border early in 1490 and encouraged a revolt in Guadix. The most successful of these operations were led by Mûsa Ibn Abu'l-Gazân, who is said to have been from a proud Moorish family with royal connections, and was perhaps a member of the Banû al-Sarrâj clan. For his part Fernando did not respond immediately. Instead he ordered the Count of Tendilla to strengthen the

frontier fortresses. Spanish forces now included a large number of allied Moorish as well as Castilian *mudejar* troops who acted as guides and vital sources of information. In May Fernando led a raiding force across the bridge at Piños Puente. Although King Fernando was able to knight his young son Prince Juan within sight of the Alhambra, the Spanish did not escape unscathed, for Mûsa Ibn Abu'l-Gazân ambushed the Marquis of Villena in a small valley, the marquis being hit by a javelin which resulted in him writing left-handed for the rest of his life. Fernando's men were still ravaging the Vega of Granada when their Moorish allies under Sîdi Yahyâ al-Naiyâr, pretending to be Muhammad XII's men, returned from a raid and seized the castle of Roma. This was then handed over to Fernando, though Sîdi Yahyâ first allowed its garrison to return to Granada. Al-Zagal similarly brought troops to support Fernando, though less willingly.

Once the Spanish raiders crossed back over the bridge at Piños Puente, Muhammad XII and Mûsa Ibn Abu'l-Gazân emerged from Granada and on 15 June headed for Alhendin. This castle south of Granada stood at the foot of the pass which blocked the road to the coast and to Muhammad XII's only other remaining territory, the vital

food-producing Alpujarras Hills and Guadalfeo Valley. It was held by a garrison under Mendo de Quesada but fell to Mûsa Ibn Abu'l-Gazân's men within a day. Muhammad XII 'Boabdil' then took the Spanish-held castles of Maracena and Bulduy which dominated Granadan communications northwards. Other Moorish raiders wrought havoc around Quezada, but were themselves ambushed on the way home.

At the end of June and early in August Muhammad XII's troops attacked Spanish-held Salobreña in an ambitious attempt to regain control of a stretch of coastline and reopen communications with Morocco. But they were unable to take the Citadel which could be resupplied by sea. The Moors beat off a small relief force from Vélez Malaga, but could not maintain a siege as they were menaced by the large Spanish garrison in Malaga. Muhammad XII 'Boabdil' also tried to win the little port of Adra which had risen in his favour before being retaken by Sîdi Yahyâ, but again failed. All that Muhammad XII could do was ravage lands belonging to al-Zagal and Sîdi Yahyâ before hurrying back to Granada as King Fernando approached.

'The Army of Firûz' in the early 16th century *Sulwân al-Mutâ'*. Other than the somewhat fanciful elephant, the troops in this picture are a reasonable representation of a Granadan army during the final war. (Ms. 528, Library, Escorial Monastery)

BELOW 'Ayn Ahlih and Sayyidat al-Dhahab (Eye of his Family and the Golden Girl),' in the *Sulwân al-Mutâ'* illustrating the lost world of Moorish domestic life. (Ms. 528, Library, Escorial Monastery)

THE CONVERGENCE ON GRANADA, 1490-1492

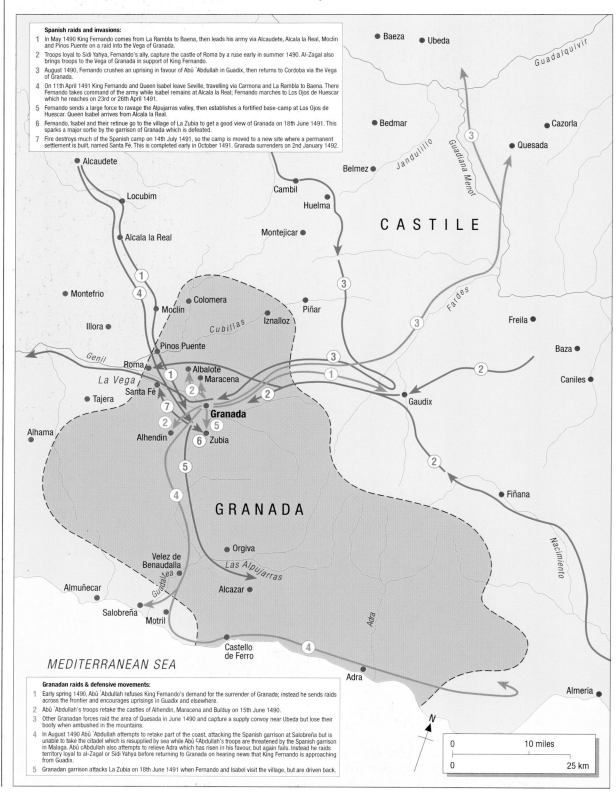

Spanish raids and invasions:

1. In May 1490 King Fernando comes from La Rambla to Baena, then leads his army via Alcaudete, Alcala la Real, Moclin and Pinos Puente on a raid into the Vega of Granada.
2. Troops loyal to Sidi Yahya, Fernando's ally, capture the castle of Roma by a ruse early in summer 1490. Al-Zagal also brings troops to the Vega of Granada in support of King Fernando.
3. August 1490, Fernando crushes an uprising in favour of Abû 'Abdullah in Guadix, then returns to Cordoba via the Vega of Granada.
4. On 11th April 1491 King Fernando and Queen Isabel leave Seville, travelling via Carmona and La Rambla to Baena. There Fernando takes command of the army while Isabel remains at Alcala la Real; Fernando marches to Los Ojos de Huescar which he reaches on 23rd or 26th April 1491.
5. Fernando sends a large force to ravage the Alpujarras valley, then establishes a fortified base-camp at Los Ojos de Huescar. Queen Isabel arrives from Alcala la Real.
6. Fernando, Isabel and their retinue go to the village of La Zubia to get a good view of Granada on 18th June 1491. This sparks a major sortie by the garrison of Granada which is defeated.
7. Fire destroys much of the Spanish camp on 14th July 1491, so the camp is moved to a new site where a permanent settlement is built, named Santa Fé. This is completed early in October 1491. Granada surrenders on 2nd January 1492.

Baeza
Ubeda
Guadalquivir
Cazorla
Bedmar
Quesada
Belmez
Jandulillo
Guadiana Menor
CASTILE
Alcaudete
Cambil
Locubim
Huelma
Freila
Alcala la Real
Montejicar
Baza
Montefrio
Fardes
Moclin
Colomera
Caniles
Ilora
Cubillas
Iznalloz
Piñar
Pinos Puente
Genil
Roma
Albalote
La Vega
Maracena
Santa Fé
Gaudix
Tajera
Granada
Alhama
Alhendin
Zubia
Fiñana
Las Alpujarras
GRANADA
Orgiva
Velez de Benaudalla
Guadalfeo
Almuñecar
Alcazar
Salobreña
Motril
Adra
Nacimiento
Castello de Ferro
MEDITERRANEAN SEA
Adra
Almeria

N

0	10 miles
0	25 km

Granadan raids & defensive movements:

1. Early spring 1490, Abû 'Abdullah refuses King Fernando's demand for the surrender of Granada; instead he sends raids across the frontier and encourages uprisings in Guadix and elsewhere.
2. Abû 'Abdullah's troops retake the castles of Alhendin, Maracena and Bulduy on 15th June 1490.
3. Other Granadan forces raid the area of Quesada in June 1490 and capture a supply convoy near Ubeda but lose their booty when ambushed in the mountains.
4. In August 1490 Abû 'Abdullah attempts to retake part of the coast, attacking the Spanish garrison at Salobreña but is unable to take the citadel which is resupplied by sea while Abû ᶜAbdullah's troops are threatened by the Spanish garrison in Malaga. Abû ᶜAbdullah also attempts to relieve Adra which has risen in his favour, but again fails. Instead he raids territory loyal to al-Zagal or Sidi Yahya before returning to Granada on hearing news that King Fernando is approaching from Guadix.
5. Granadan garrison attacks La Zubia on 18th June 1491 when Fernando and Isabel visit the village, but are driven back.

Fernando appeared in the Vega of Granada shortly after Muhammad XII returned, and spent 15 days ravaging what was left of its agricultural wealth. The winter of 1490–91 was quiet while Fernando and Isabel prepared for their final attack on the city of Granada. Meanwhile, Muhammad al-Zagal, unable to endure the humiliation of Spanish rule, sold his remaining estates and migrated to North Africa. Protests from the Mamlûk Sultan of Egypt, contrasting the good treatment enjoyed by his Christian subjects in Jerusalem with the persecution suffered by Muslims in Spain, were ignored. The Sultan did not feel inclined to do more as Egypt had recently asked for Spanish naval support against the expanding Ottoman Turks, while the Turks themselves were preoccupied with their own conquests in the Balkans. Muhammad XII's last appeal to Muhammad al-Shaykh, the ruler of Fez, received no response, and the ruler of neighbouring Tlemsen in western Algeria had already sacrificed Granada in return for trade relations with Spain.

'THE MOORS' LAST SIGH'

A very large army assembled in the Val de Velillos for the final assault. Queen Isabel went to Alcala la Real, while the king led his troops into the Vega of Granada. On 23 or 26 April the royal tent was erected near a spring at a place identified as Los Ojos de Huescar which may have been the modern Ogijares. Fernando's first action was to send the Marquis of Vellena to the Alpujarras. The king soon followed with the rest of the army, their task being to stop this fertile region supplying Granada with

The doubled walls leading down from the Gibralfaro fortress to the Alcazaba fortified governor's palace overlooking the city of Malaga, designed to maintain communication between the city and the fortress. (Author's photograph)

food. Twenty-four towns and villages were ransacked before the army returned to build a fortified camp facing Granada over the Rio Genil.

In the Moorish capital Muhammad XII's chief *wazîr* or prime minister, Abû'l-Qâsim 'Abd al-Mâlik said that there was only food for a few months and that they should seek the best surrender terms available, while Mûsa Ibn Abû'l-Gazân argued in favour of resistance. Muhammad XII 'Boabdil' agreed, and the result was an eight-month siege which eventually degenerated into little more than a blockade with few active operations by either side. Queen Isabel and her children arrived at Los Ojos de Huescar once the camp was complete, but as Fernando made no attempt to attack Granada, Mûsa Ibn Abû'l-Gazân ordered that some of the gates be left open to tempt the enemy. According to a perhaps legendary account he said: *'Our bodies will bar the gates. We have nothing to fight for but the ground we stand on. Without that we are without home or country.'* He also encouraged his men to skirmish with the enemy, ambush them when possible, and challenge the Spanish knights to individual combat. For some time the proud Spanish élite responded, but they lost so many of their best men that King Fernando eventually banned further duels. This was hard for the knights to accept, as the Moors now came close to their encampment, taunting the Spaniards for skulking behind ditches. These tactics cost the Moors heavily in horses, however, and by the end of the siege they were down to only a few hundred mounts.

During this stage of the siege several episodes caught the attention of chroniclers. For example, a young knight named Fernando Perez de Pulgar took advantage of Mûsa's open gate policy and, with 15 companions, broke through a poorly guarded postern, galloped up the sleeping streets and pinned a tablet with the words 'Ave Maria' to the door of a mosque before escaping.

The main clash came on 18 June 1491 when Isabel wanted to see the famous Alhambra Palace. Fernando and a substantial force under the Marquis of Cadiz escorted her to the village of La Zubia which had a good view, but their banners sparked a major sortie which included Moorish infantry and field artillery. Fernando and Isabel were watching from a window when the Moors emerged, dragging their small cannon. Among them was a horseman named Tarîf who had Pulgar's plaque with

The small fortified market town of Xauen high in the Rif Mountains of northern Morocco was rebuilt by refugees from the Amirate of Granada even before Granada fell to the Spaniards. (Author's photograph)

CAVALRY DUEL OUTSIDE GRANADA DURING THE FINAL SIEGE

During the first months of the siege of Granada, Moorish cavalry came out of the city and challenged their foes to individual combat. At first the Christian knights responded, but so many Spanish were killed that King Fernando banned further participation. Fernando and Isabel were products of the Renaissance which had now spread to Spain. For them, wars were fought to be won, not as an arena for personal glory as might have been the case during previous centuries.

Gunport in one of the eastern towers of the fortification of Ronda. It is an example of how the Moors of Granada tried, despite their limited resources, to keep up with the latest technological developments. (Author's photograph)

the words 'Ave Maria' tied to his horse's tail. This was too much for the young knight who begged for permission to accept the challenge. In the duel which followed, Tarîf was killed.

At first the rest of the Spanish troops obeyed Fernando's order not to provoke combat, but when the guns began to fire the Marquis ordered his men to charge. Cavalry led by Muhammad XII 'Boabdil' and Mûsa Ibn Abu'l-Gazân defended their infantry as best they could before the Moors were forced back within their walls. Almost a month later fire destroyed half of the Spanish camp, including Queen Isabel's tent, and the Spanish launched a large raid to stop the Moors taking advantage of it. Muhammad XII and Mûsa Ibn 'Abd al-Malik attacked the raiders, but the Amir was almost captured. It was their final sally.

Now Fernando and Isabel built a permanent siege encampment of stone and mortar west of Granada to give their army shelter during the winter. It was completed early in October and given the name of Santa Fé. This finally convinced the Amir that resistance was hopeless and negotiations began the same month. They were conducted on the Moorish side by the *wazîr* Abû'l Qâsim 'Abd al-Mâlik, and on the Spanish side by Fernando de Zafra, the royal secretary, and Gonzalo de Cordoba, who had wide experience of Granadan affairs. The negotiations were kept secret as Muhammad XII was not sure how the people of Granada would react, and the Amir may even have been in touch with the enemy since the start of the siege. Terms were agreed on 22 November and were ratified three days later. They were surprisingly generous to the defeated Moors: virtually all their terms being accepted simply because Spain was exhausted by war, winter was approaching and Fernando feared that disease would ruin their army. Their sights may also already have been elsewhere.

Muhammad XII was now extremely unpopular in Granada. The inhabitants had got wind of the negotiations and regarded their Amir as a traitor. So the surrender date was hurried forward. Muhammad XII was offered the rich but rugged Alpujarras region, which would have been

78

difficult to conquer, and his main lieutenants were richly rewarded. Nevertheless, Mûsa Ibn Abû'l-Gazân is said to have refused to take part, riding out of Granada fully armed and was never seen again. According to legends, Mûsa challenged a group of Spanish knights near the Rio Genil, killing several before, desperately wounded, he threw himself into the river and disappeared.

On 1 January 1492, Muhammad XII sent 500 hostages and asked for Spanish troops to enter the Alhambra secretly the following night to protect him from his own people. The next day the city surrendered, and four days later Fernando and Isabel made their formal entry. The Christian cross, the royal standard and banner of the Order of Santiago were raised over the Alhambra as 'Boabdil' handed over the keys of the city and the royal herald shouted: *'Santiago, Santiago, Santiago! Castilla, Castilla, Castilla! For the very High and Puissant Lords Don Fernando and Doña Isabel who have won the city of Granada and its whole kingdom by force of arms from the infidel Moors!'* Everyone recognised the importance of this date which, according to one Spanish chronicler, was *'the most signal and blessed day there has ever been in Spain'*. According to a Muslim chronicler, however, it was *'one of the most terrible catastrophes which have befallen Islam'*. According to legend 'Boabdil' wept as he rode over the mountain pass south of Granada, at which his mother the formidable Fâtima said, *'You may well weep like a woman for what you could not defend like a man.'* It is still known as the Puerto del Suspiro del More, the Pass of the Moor's Sigh.

The gardens of the Generalife, *Jinnat al-'Arif* or 'High Garden' overlooking the Alhambra. It is still famous for the magnificent gardens, fountains and pools which were the delight of the Nasrid ruling élite. (Author's photograph)

Boabdil surrendering the keys of Granada to King Fernando in 1492. Though hardly a realistic illustration of the event, this carved choir stall captures the triumph of the Spanish king and the humiliation of Muhammad XII, last Amir of Granada. (*In situ*, Choir of the Cathedral, Toledo)

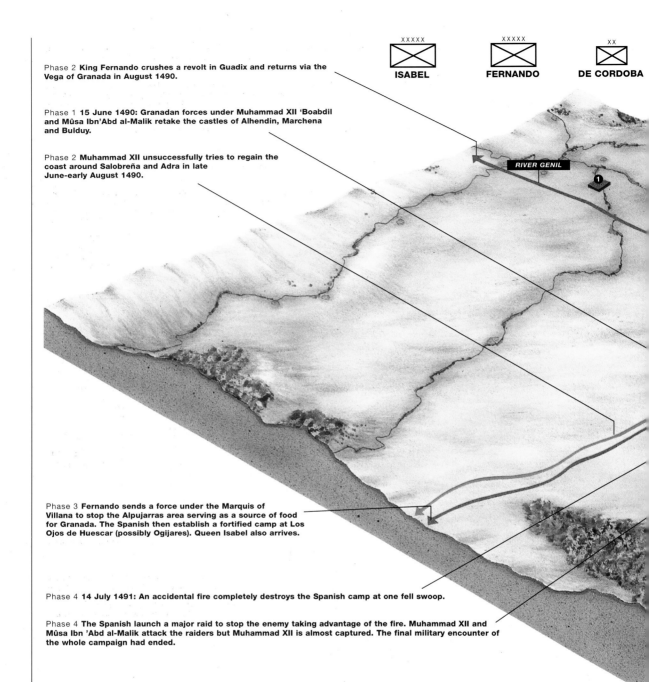

Phase 2 **King Fernando crushes a revolt in Guadix and returns via the Vega of Granada in August 1490.**

Phase 1 **15 June 1490: Granadan forces under Muhammad XII 'Boabdil and Mûsa Ibn'Abd al-Malik retake the castles of Alhendin, Marchena and Bulduy.**

Phase 2 **Muhammad XII unsuccessfully tries to regain the coast around Salobreña and Adra in late June-early August 1490.**

ISABEL   FERNANDO   DE CORDOBA

RIVER GENIL

1

Phase 3 **Fernando sends a force under the Marquis of Villana to stop the Alpujarras area serving as a source of food for Granada. The Spanish then establish a fortified camp at Los Ojos de Huescar (possibly Ogijares). Queen Isabel also arrives.**

Phase 4 **14 July 1491: An accidental fire completely destroys the Spanish camp at one fell swoop.**

Phase 4 **The Spanish launch a major raid to stop the enemy taking advantage of the fire. Muhammad XII and Mûsa Ibn 'Abd al-Malik attack the raiders but Muhammad XII is almost captured. The final military encounter of the whole campaign had ended.**

THE FALL OF GRANADA (JUNE 1490-JANUARY 1492)

Viewed from the south-west. With no sea access, her agricultural wealth destroyed, and now abandoned by her North African allies, Granada awaited the final onslaught. The Spanish laid siege for over a year with small sporadic attacks launched by either side. Once a permanent encampment of stone was erected by Fernando however, Muhammad XII had to face surrender or the complete annihilation of his people.

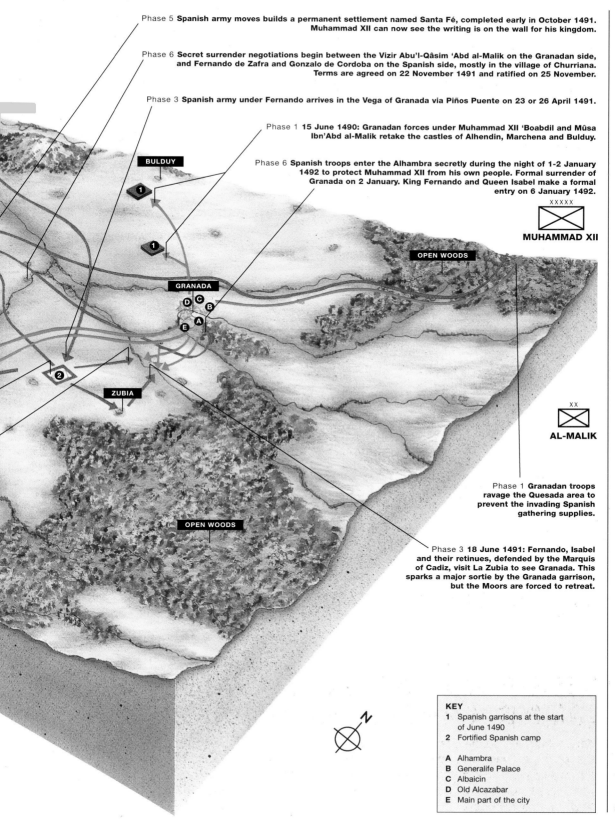

Phase 5 **Spanish army moves builds a permanent settlement named Santa Fé, completed early in October 1491. Muhammad XII can now see the writing is on the wall for his kingdom.**

Phase 6 **Secret surrender negotiations begin between the Vizir Abu'l-Qâsim 'Abd al-Malik on the Granadan side, and Fernando de Zafra and Gonzalo de Cordoba on the Spanish side, mostly in the village of Churriana. Terms are agreed on 22 November 1491 and ratified on 25 November.**

Phase 3 **Spanish army under Fernando arrives in the Vega of Granada via Piños Puente on 23 or 26 April 1491.**

Phase 1 **15 June 1490: Granadan forces under Muhammad XII 'Boabdil and Mûsa Ibn'Abd al-Malik retake the castles of Alhendin, Marchena and Bulduy.**

Phase 6 **Spanish troops enter the Alhambra secretly during the night of 1-2 January 1492 to protect Muhammad XII from his own people. Formal surrender of Granada on 2 January. King Fernando and Queen Isabel make a formal entry on 6 January 1492.**

BULDUY

XXXXX
MUHAMMAD XII

OPEN WOODS

GRANADA

D C B
E A

ZUBIA

XX
AL-MALIK

OPEN WOODS

Phase 1 **Granadan troops ravage the Quesada area to prevent the invading Spanish gathering supplies.**

Phase 3 **18 June 1491: Fernando, Isabel and their retinues, defended by the Marquis of Cadiz, visit La Zubia to see Granada. This sparks a major sortie by the Granada garrison, but the Moors are forced to retreat.**

KEY
1 Spanish garrisons at the start of June 1490
2 Fortified Spanish camp

A Alhambra
B Generalife Palace
C Albaicin
D Old Alcazabar
E Main part of the city

83

AFTERMATH AND RECKONING

UNIFICATION AND THE DAWN OF EMPIRE

King Fernando and Queen Isabel used their victory to promote the concept of Spanish unity. In purely military terms Spanish armies also learned a great deal between 1481 and 1492, not only in the use of firearms but in the management of very large forces, as well as combined operations involving land forces supplied by sea while inside enemy territory. Not surprisingly, therefore, the armies of Spain became a force to be reckoned with in early 16th century Europe and to an even greater degree on the other side of the Atlantic. Here, many aspects of the frontier society which evolved in Castile and Aragon reappeared in South and Central America.

The year 1492 saw Granada fall, Columbus set sail and the General Edict of Expulsion of Jews from both Castile and Aragon. The Muslims of Iberia survived for considerably longer, though they too would eventually suffer the same fate. More immediately, plans were drawn up to invade North Africa. Not only was North Africa seen as 'the road to Jerusalem', but its conquest would recreate what was believed to have been the ancient Visigothic kingdom and, of more practical value, it would bring the Spaniards closer to the sources of African gold which had dazzled Europeans for centuries.

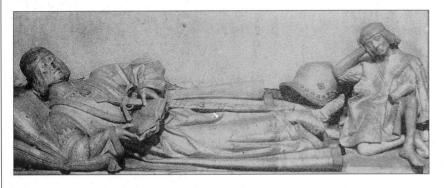

Tomb of Don Iñigo López de Mendoza, Count of Tendilla and first Captain General of Granada, who played a significant role during the conquest of Granada. (Church of San Ginés, Guadalajara)

THE RUIN OF IBERIAN ISLAM

The reasons for Granada's defeat were clearly described in a letter sent to the Ottoman Sultan Bayazit a few years later, by which time Spanish oppression had shown Muslims the magnitude of their disaster: *'The Christians attacked us from all sides in a vast torrent, company after company, smiting us with zeal and resolution like locusts in the multitude of their cavalry and weapons... When we became weak, they camped in our territory and smote us,*

The Alpujarra Hills overlooking the Rio Guadalfeo at Orgiva, south-east of Granada. Muhammad XII was given several villages in this region following his surrender of Granada. (Author's photograph)

FROM LEFT TO RIGHT
1,2, **Spanish *armet*, late 15th century (ex- Baron de Cosson Collection). 3, Spanish or Portuguese *salet* with a very long 'tail' to protect the back of the neck (Rainer Daehnhardt Collection, Lisbon). 4, 15th century Spanish *salet*. There would probably have been separate ear-defences attached to the side (ex-Pauilhac Collection). 5, Spanish *cabacete* or war-hat with a decorative band, 15th century. (ex-Pauilhac Collection)**

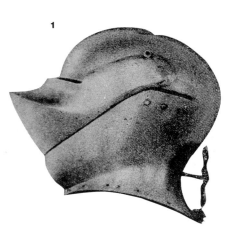

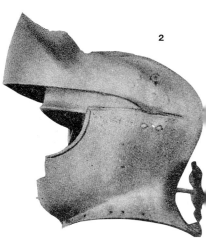

Baptism of Moorish women in Granada in an early 16th century carved wooden panel. The forced conversion of the Muslim population of Granada was in direct contravention of the agreed surrender terms. (*In situ*, Cathedral, Granada)

town after town, bringing up many large cannons that demolished the impregnable walls of the towns, attacking them energetically during the siege for many months and days, with zeal and determination...'

Although the surrender terms offered to Muhammad XII were generous, the Amir had to hand over his state to Fernando and Isabel, and in return they allowed him to hold three 'towns', or more correctly villages in the Alpujarras, Val de Guadalfeo and Val de Puchena as their vassal. From the Spanish point of view this had the added benefit of avoiding the need to conquer the rugged mountains south-east of Granada. Within a few months Muhammad XII's wife, 'Ali al-'Attar's daughter known as Morayma in Spanish sources, reportedly died and was buried at Mondújar. According to the *Life of Cardinal Medoza*, however, Muhammad XII's wife went to Madrid with her children and converted to Christianity. In October 1493 the ex-Amir himself sold his 'towns' to the Spanish crown and went to Tlemsen in what is now western Algeria, from where he and his remaining followers eventually made their way to Fez. Muhammad XII was around 80 years of age when he died in battle, fighting in support of the Sultan of Fez in 1536. As the Spanish chronicler Màrmol put it: '*with him was Muley Abi Abdallah el Zogoibi, king that*

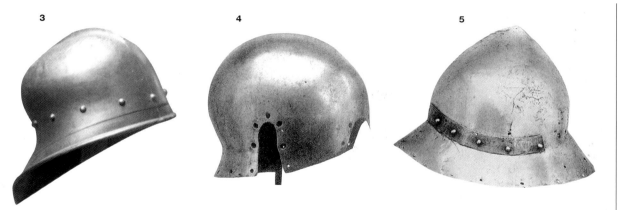

3   4   5

was of Granada... In this battle el Zogoibi died, which made a mockery of Fortune, for death struck him as he was defending the kingdom of somebody else when he had not dared defend his own.'

Muhammad XIII al-Zagal had already sold his estates and crossed over the Tlemsen when he died in 1494. The turbulent Banû al-Sarrâj family similarly moved from Granada to the Alpujarras but, like much of the old Muslim élite, they found their new situation intolerable and departed for Morocco in March 1493. One little-known military leader named 'Abd al'Hassan 'Ali al-Manzari arrived with a small number refugees, rebuilt the town of Titwân and forged an alliance with 'Abd al-Hassan the Sharifian leader in nearby Xauen.

ABOVE **A two-masted galley on a painted bowl from Rabat in Morocco, 14th-15th centuries. It shows a very stylised ship, perhaps an early version of the *chebeque* in which embittered refugees from Granada wrought havoc on Christian shipping in the 16th century. (Museum of Moroccan Art, Rabat)**

Four 15th century Moorish and Hispano-Moresque daggers of the so-called 'ear dagger' style which originated in Granada or North Africa if not further east. (Museo Nazionale de Bargello, Florence)

THE BATTLEFIELDS TODAY

Southern Spain is one of Europe's main holiday areas and its coast has almost become one long beach resort. A few kilometres inland, however, many areas remain difficult to reach and, except for the main towns such as Granada, Ronda, Cordoba and Seville, hotels are surprisingly few. Camp-sites exist but are mostly concentrated along the coast, and some wilder mountain regions can still only be reached with a four-wheel-drive vehicle or on foot.

Nevertheless, the area of the old Amirate of Granada was relatively small and most campaigns took place around the main towns, in the cultivated Vegas, or along the coast. The only times large armies operated in the higher hills was while trying to cross them via relatively few passes which are essentially the same as those followed by modern roads.

As elsewhere in Europe, the main cities of southern Spain have expanded far beyond their medieval extent and the view of Granada from the Alhambra Palace is not that seen by Boabdil. Another feature of what had been the Muslim Amirate of Granada cannot be found anywhere in Spain and that is the bustling and exciting character of a medieval Islamic city. The traveller must cross the Strait of Gibraltar to Morocco to find this lost world. But in Fez he or she can enter a living relic from the world of medieval Islam, for although Fez played little part in events surrounding the fall of Granada, a walk through the narrow shaded streets of its old quarter will take the visitor right back to medieval Granada.

Hispano-Moresque or Moorish stirrup, late 15th century. (ex-Lady Ludlow Collection)

Hispano-Moresque stirrups, late 15th century. (Inv. Pierpoint Morgan Gift, 17.190.641-642, Metropolitan Museum of Art, New York)

Part of a late 15th century Moorish or Hispano-Moresque bridle. (British Museum, London)

St James fighting the Moors at the battle of Clavijo, from the Retáblo da Vida e da Ordem de Santiago, Portuguese early 16th century. Here St James is dressed as a senior member of the Military Order of Santiago. (Museu Nacional de Arte Antiga, Lisbon)

Early 16th century Tunisian saddle with a small drum attached to the front. (Inv. F-46, Real Armeria, Madrid)

CHRONOLOGY

1461	'Alî Abû'l-Hassan 'Alî becomes Amir of Granada.
1462	Granada loses Gibraltar and Archidona.
1462–72	Peasant revolt and civil war in Aragon; major rebellion against Marînid rulers of Morocco.
1469	Marriage of Princess Isabel of Castile and Prince Fernando of Aragon.
1471	Portuguese take Arzila and Tangier.
1472	Muhammad al-Shaykh becomes first Wattasid ruler of central Morocco.
1474	Death of King Enrique IV of Castile; succeeded by Queen Isabel.
1475	Peasant revolt in Kingdom of Aragon.
1478	Truce between Castile and Granada.
1479	Death of King Juan II of Aragon; succeeded by Fernando II (1479–1516); Castile and Aragon united under the joint rule of Isabel and Fernando.
1481 (Dec 26)	Granadans seize Zahara.
1482 (Feb 28)	Castilians seize Alhama; (March–July) unsuccessful Moorish attempts to retake Alhama; (July 15) Abû'l-Hassan defeats Fernando's attempt to take Loja; Abû'l-Hassan toppled by a palace coup in favour of his son Muhammad XII in Granada, who establishes rival capital in Malaga.
1483	Congress of leaders of the Castilian *Hermandad* to reform this organisation; (March–April) Castilians defeated in the mountains behind Malaga; (April 20) Muhammad XII captured during an unsuccessful raid against Lucena; released after making a treaty with Fernando and Isabel; Abû'l-Hassan regains Granada; (September 17) Granadan raid towards Cordoba defeated at Lopera; (October) Granadan legal authorities deny Muhammad XII's right to the throne; Castilians retake Zahara.
1484	Spanish fleets sent to patrol Strait of Gibraltar; Genoa and Venice threatened with reprisals if they help Granada; large Castilian raid as far as the Mediterranean coast; (June) Fernando takes Alora and Setenil; (late summer) Castilian raid into the Vega of Granada.
1485 (January)	*Auto da Fé* in Seville burns 19 men and women, making total of 500 *conversos* convicted as heretics; Abû'l-Hassan incapacitated by a stroke and replaced by his brother Muhammad al-Zagal as Muhammad XIII; Watasid ruler of Fez makes a treaty of friend-

The Fortress Hill on Mount Acho overlooking Ceuta which forms a Spanish enclave on the northern coast of Morocco, having fallen to the Portuguese in 1415. (Author's photograph)

ship with Spain; (spring) Castilians take Coin and Cartama, raid Malaga area, take Ronda and Marbella; Granadan raid into the area of Medina Sidonia; unsuccessful Castilian attempt to take Moclin is diverted to take Cambil and Albahar; Muhammad XII returns to Granada with Castilian support; civil war in Granada between Muhammad XII 'Boabdil' and Muhammad XIII al-Zagal; (February) al-Zagal takes Almeria from Muhammad XII who flees to Castile.

1486 Reconciliation between Muhammad XII and Muhammad XIII; (June) Castilians take Loja and capture Muhammad XII, also take Illora and Moclin; Castilians raid Granada and defeat Muslim sortie at Pinos Puente, but then suffer serious losses outside Granada; another treaty signed between Muhammad XII, and Fernando and Isabel; (September 15) Muhammad XII regains city of Granada with Castilian help but al-Zagal retains the Alhambra;

1487 (April 27) Fernando takes Vélez Malaga; Muhammad al-Zagal loses support in Granada and goes to Almeria; (May) third treaty signed by Muhammad XII 'Boabdil', Fernando and Isabel; (August) Castilians take Malaga.

1488 Early in the year Spanish forces help the Duke of Brittany against the Regent of France but are defeated; political difficulties within Castile and Aragon; Fernando invades the eastern Amirate of Granada, taking Vera, but is driven off by al-Zagal's garrisons; several counter-raids by al-Zagal's forces into Castile.

1489 (August) Muhammad al-Shaykh, ruler of Fez, forces Portuguese to abandon the building of a fortress near Wadi Lukkus, then renews his peace treaty with Portugal; plagues and floods in Andalusian Castile; (December) Castilians take Cuxar and Baza; peace treaty between Muhammad XIII al-Zagal, Fernando and Isabel.

1490 Muhammad XII refuses to surrender Granada, authorises counter-raids, retakes Alhendin (Jun 15), encourages revolt in Guadix, unsuccessfully attempts to take Salobreña and Adra; Castilians raid the Vega of Granada and crush rebellion in Guadix.

1491 (April 26) Start of the final siege of Granada; (July) Castilian siege camp outside Granada is burned down and replaced by a permanent town named Santa Fé; (November 15) surrender agreement ratified by Granada and Spanish rulers.

1492 (Night of Jan 1–2) Spanish troops enter the Alhambra; official surrender of Granada the following day; (January 6) Fernando and Isabel enter Granada.

FURTHER READING

Alcocer Martinez, M., *Castillos y fortalezas del antique reine de Granada* (Tangier 1941).

Amador de los Rios y Villalta, R., 'Notas acerca de la batalla de Lucera de la prision de Boabdul in 1483,' *Revista des archives, bibliotecas y museos*, XVI (1906).

Arié, R., 'Quelques remarques sur le Costume des Musulmans d'Espagne au Temps des Nasrîds,' *Arabica*, XII (1965).
   L'Espagne Musulmane au Temps des Nasrides (1232-1492), (Paris 1973).
   L'Occident Musulman au Bas Moyen Age (Paris 1992).

Bazzana, A., 'Fortresses du Royaume nasride de Grenade (XIIIe-XVe siècle): la défense des frontières,' *Chateau Gaillard*, XI (1983).

Brett, M. and W. Forman, *The Moors, Islam in the West* (London 1980).

Calvert, A.F., *Spanish Arms and Armour* (London 1908).

De Mata Carriazo, J., *Los Relieves de la Guerra de Granada en la Silleria del Coro de la Catedral de Toledo* (Granada 1985).
   'Asiento de la cosas de Ronda, Conquista y repartiment de la cuidad por los reyes catolicos (1485-1491),' *Miscelanea de Estudios Arabes y Hebraicos*, III (1954).
   'Cartas de la frontera de Granada,' *Andalus*, XI (1946).
   'Relaciones fronterizas entre Jaen y Granada en el ano 1479,' *Revista de Archivos, Bibliotecas y Museos*, LXI (1955).
   'Un alcalde entre los cristianos y los moros, en la fronters de Granada,' *Andalus*, XIII (1948).

De Riquer, M., *L'Arnès del Cavaller: Armes I Armadues catalanes medievals* (Barcelona 1968).

Edwards, J., 'Hostages and Ransomers,' *Medieval World*, VIII (Jan-Feb 1993).

Eguaras, A.M., L.S. Pérez and E. De Santiago-Simón, 'La Ballesta Naza del Museo Arqueologico de Granada,' *Cuadernos de la Alhambra*, XVIII (1982).

Fernández-Armestro, F., *Ferdinand and Isabella* (London 1975).

Fisher, G., *Barbary Legend: War, Trade and Piracy in North Africa 1415-1830* (Oxford 1957).

Gala, A., *Granada de los nazaries* (Barcelona 1994).

Garcia Fuentes, J.M., 'Las armas hispano-musulmanas al final de la Reconquista,' *Cronica Nova*, III (1969).

Glick, T.F., *From Muslim Fortress to Christian Castle, Social and Cultural Change in Medieval Spain* (Manchester 1995).

Harvey, L., *Islamic Spain, 1250 to 1550* (London 1990).

Hillgarth, J.N., *The Spanish Kingdoms 1250-1516* (Oxford 1976-78).

Huici, A. (edit), *Coleccion de cronicas arabes de la Reconquista* (Tetuan 1952-55).

Jayyusi, S.K. (edit), *The Legacy of Muslim Spain* (Leiden 1992).

Ladero Quesada, M.A., 'La defense de Granada a raiz de la conquista, Cominezos de un problema,' *Miscelanea de Estudios Arabes y Hebraicos,* XVI-XVII (1967-8).

Andalucia en el Siglo XV, Estudios de Historia Politica (Madrid 1973).

Castilla y la Conquista del Reino de Granada (Valladolid 1967).

Granada, Historia de un País Islámico (1232-1571) (Granada 1969).

Lafuente Alcantara, M., *Historia de Granada* (Granada 1845; reprint Granada 1992).

Lanuza Cano, F., *El Ejército en tiempo de los Reyes Católicos* (Madrid 1953).

Liss, P.K., *Isabel the Queen* (Oxford 1992).

López de Coca Castañer, J.E., 'Institutions on the Castilian-Granadan Frontier, 1369-1482,' in R. Bartlett and A. MacKay (edits.), *Medieval Frontier Societies* (Oxford 1989).

Mackay, A., *Society, Economy and Religion in Late Medieval Castile* (London 1987).

Mann, J.G., 'Notes on the Armour worn in Spain from the Tenth to the Fifteenth Century,' *Archaeologia,* LXXIII (1933).

Prescott, W.H., edited and with Introduction by A.D. McJoynt, *The Art of War in Spain, The Conquest of Granada 1481-1492* (London 1995).

Russell, P.E., *Portugal, Spain and the African Atlantic 1343-1490* (London 1995).

Santaella, R.G.P. and J.E.L. De Coco Castañer, *Historia de Granada, vol. II: La Epoca Medieval, Siglos VIII-XV* (Granada 1987).

Seco de Lucena Paredes, L., 'La Sultana Madre de Boabdil,' *Andalus,* XII (1947).

Terrasse, H., 'Les forteresses de l'Espagne musulmane,' *Boletin de la Real Academia de la Historia,* CXXXIV (1954).

Vigón, J., *El Ejército de los Reyes Católicos* (Madrid 1968).

Viguera Molins, M.J., *De las Taifas al reino de Granada. Al-Andalus, siglos XI-XV* (Madrid 1995).

Villanueva, C., 'Rabitas granadinas,' *Miscelanea de Estudios Arabes y Hebraicos,* III (1954).

INDEX

Figures in **bold** refer to illustrations

COMPANION SERIES FROM OSPREY

MEN-AT-ARMS

An unrivalled source of information on the organisation, uniforms and equipment of the world's fighting men, past and present. The series covers hundreds of subjects spanning 5,000 years of history. Each 48-page book includes concise texts packed with specific information, some 40 photos, maps and diagrams, and eight colour plates of uniformed figures.

ELITE

Detailed information on the uniforms and insignia of the world's most famous military forces. Each 64-page book contains some 50 photographs and diagrams, and 12 pages of full-colour artwork.

NEW VANGUARD

Comprehensive histories of the design, development and operational use of the world's armoured vehicles and artillery. Each 48-page book contains eight pages of full-colour artwork including a detailed cutaway.

WARRIOR

Definitive analysis of the armour, weapons, tactics and motivation of the fighting men of history. Each 64-page book contains cutaways and exploded artwork of the warrior's weapons and armour.

ORDER OF BATTLE

The most detailed information ever published on the units which fought history's great battles. Each 96-page book contains comprehensive organisation diagrams supported by ultra-detailed colour maps. Each title also includes a large fold-out base map.

AIRCRAFT OF THE ACES

Focuses exclusively on the elite pilots of major air campaigns, and includes unique interviews with surviving aces sourced specifically or each volume. Each 96-page volume contains up to 40 specially commissioned artworks, unit listings, new scale plans and the best archival photography available.

COMBAT AIRCRAFT

Technical information from the world's leading aviation writers on the aircraft types flown. Each 96-page volume contains up to 40 specially commissioned artworks, unit listings, new scale plans and the best archival photography available.